A Short History of
WESTERN CANADA

A Short History of
WESTERN CANADA

J. W. GRANT MacEWAN.

B.S.A., M.S., LL.D.
Lieutenant-Governor of Alberta

MAXWELL FORAN

Assistant Principal
Greenview School, Calgary

McGRAW-HILL RYERSON LIMITED

Toronto • Montreal • New York • London • Sydney • Mexico
Johannesburg • Panama • Düsseldorf • Singapore • São Paulo
Kuala Lumpur • New Delhi

A SHORT HISTORY OF WESTERN CANADA

This book was first published in hardcover under the title WEST TO THE SEA.

ISBN 0-07-077787-X

1 2 3 4 5 6 7 8 9 10   AP   3 2 1 0 9 8 7 6 5 4

Printed and bound in Canada

Contents

Preface   vi

1 / The Bountiful Land — Its Early Inhabitants   1

2 / Furs — The West's First Industry   22

3 / Pioneers and Adventurers   39

4 / Confederation and the West   67

5 / The Law on Horseback   80

6 / The Railways and the Land Rush   93

7 / The West Enters the Twentieth Century   114

8 / The Canadian West Today   134

Index   164

Preface

British Columbia, Alberta, Saskatchewan, and Manitoba are young provinces in a young country, on a young continent, that is, young as compared with the length of human occupancy in other parts of the world.

Man himself, of course, is a relatively young creature; he has been on this planet only 10 or 20 million years. This may seem a long time, but such things as water, soil, trees, and many forms of animals were here long before man made his appearance. His entry into this world was like a family moving to a new house which members of the family had no part in planning, building, or furnishing. Yet, although they had nothing to do with the making of their world, as good "tenants" they could be expected to assume quite a lot of responsibility for looking after it. It is the duty of all present tenants to keep it as a fit place in which to live for a long time to come.

The western Canadian provinces were among the last of those new "houses" into which man moved. This fact should bring special interest. History is largely a study of what people have done with their lands, or houses, and the good things in Nature, or "furnishings". Western Canadian history is an individual study of man's occupation of particular new houses. Before turning our attention to regional history, however, it would be well to think about the things man has always needed with his houses, and then to consider how the provinces concerned fared in the matter of furnishings.

Air is one of the few human needs nearly always present in abundance, but it would be a mistake to take air for granted. Although modern man has been successful in bringing air conditioning to homes and offices, he has not been as successful in keeping the air over his big cities in such a clean and healthful state. Many people in crowded communities are justifiably worried about the dangers resulting from air pollution.

Other essentials, such as soil and water, should not be taken for granted either. Drinking water is a daily requirement for people and animals and, without both water and soil, there could be neither grain, grass, nor vegetable crops. Throughout history, where soil and water were present together, people generally flourished, thus explaining why people chose, in so many cases, to live along the big rivers of the world and went to war over the best locations. This combination of soil and water explains one of the early attractions in certain parts of the western provinces.

Much has been written about the discovery of the Americas and the Spanish seamen who crossed the Atlantic, claiming territory in the New World for Spain. The Spanish adventurers' chief concern was treasure. There was much of it, and the Spaniards loaded ships with silver and gold and sent the wealth to their homeland.

Spain's decline as a nation was partly due to her failure to use the wealth she received from the New World wisely. Gold and silver alone do not make a country rich. History helps to explain this. At home, Spain lacked the two essentials for continued power and progress: ample water and good soil, and all the rich plunder from across the Atlantic could not ensure continued greatness.

A country or province is not likely to be any richer than its inhabitants make it. With this in mind, the importance of other natural resources must be noted.

What is a natural resource? It is easier to give examples than definitions. The soil, water, and clean air mentioned previously are the essential natural resources. A resource is something from which it is possible to draw benefit in time of need, something capable of making life easier, happier, or more comfortable. It is a little like a money-box full of currency which can be used when needed. The resources of water, soil, and clean air are needed at all times. Forests, minerals, oil, gas, potash, parklands, native animals, and waterpower are the additional resources certain to be of value to a country and its people. Man in any area is likely to use as many resources as possible, always trying to produce more and make his way of life more comfortable.

Therefore, in approaching western Canadian history, one should take note of the extent and character of the area's resources, remembering that it was a knowledge of only part of this natural wealth which brought men there in the first place. In this way, it may be seen how an increasing number of discoveries shaped the history of these provinces. Only then is it possible to imagine how far the future of the area will be determined by the uses to which the resources are directed.

Yet history has words of warning: in the past, the record of fallen civilizations has been the history of man's abuse of the resource furnishings of his houses. An individual can only spend what he has in his money-box and no more. The more he has, the greater the task of managing it wisely. The history of other lands offers many reminders. Now, let us examine these Canadian houses and their furnishings of natural treasure in greater detail and see how the tenants have conducted themselves.

1 The Bountiful Land — Its Early Inhabitants

The Rich Gifts of Nature

Like a father making handsome gifts to his children, Nature was generous to the western provinces. Considered in terms of history, living space, climate, scenery, and natural resources, western Canadians received a very rich inheritance, and one calling for thanksgiving. People in many crowded and less fortunate parts of the world would look on them with envy.

The first feature to impress itself upon explorers and traders in the early West was the tremendous size of the country. Men travelling by ox-drawn carts on the thousand-mile journey between Fort Garry, now Winnipeg, and Fort Edmonton, had the feeling of being on a trail which had no end.

Like the rest of Canada, the prairie, parkland, and mountain country which became Manitoba, Saskatchewan, Alberta, and British Columbia continued to offer living space in abundance. With a north-south depth of 756 miles and a combined width of more than 1,200 miles, the total area of the four provinces is over a million square miles. After Quebec, British Columbia is the biggest province in land area, then Ontario, Alberta, Saskatchewan, and Manitoba.

Each of these western provinces is bigger than Spain or Sweden, twice as big as New Zealand, Italy, or the United Kingdom, five times as big as Greece, fifteen times as big as Denmark, and twenty-two times as big as Belgium.

On the basis of 1966 population, the land area of the Canadian West is sufficiently extensive to allow an average of 130 acres of surface space for every man, woman, and child. It corresponds with the population density of the whole of Canada, that is, about five persons per square mile. Such an amount of room is almost beyond the imagination of people in other lands. With the world population now above three billion, overcrowding is a serious problem in many countries. Residents in lands where the population exceeds 500 per square mile must look longingly at the relatively unoccupied areas of this country. The Canadian figures, of course, could be misleading for the simple reason that much of the country's surface, such as the Yukon and the Northwest Territories, is not capable of supporting more than a sparsely scattered population.

In the homestead years, most western people lived on farms. With a trend toward fewer and bigger farms, however, the population balance changed until half of Manitoba's people lived in Metropolitan Winnipeg and half of Alberta's population was in Edmonton and Calgary. Almost half of the British Columbia population was found in Metropolitan Vancouver. The rapidly growing cities quickly developed into industrial centres.

While the earliest white men in the country recognized the great spaces, many of them misjudged the climate, thinking it would discourage settlement. Fur traders spoke in scornful terms, calling it the land of ice and snow.

The West certainly has its share of ice and snow, but the weather, as experienced over an entire year, justifies the conclusion that the country has an attractive climate. An unusual degree of change and variety has its own merit. Canadians becoming residents in some more southerly regions where ice and snow and chilly days do not occur have been known to complain about monotony when the weather was approximately the same day after day, month after month.

With insulated houses and modern heating methods, western winters can be pleasant and, with regard to winter sports like skating, hockey, curling, tobogganing, and skiing, winters can be fun. In spite of remarks once stating that the severity of northwestern winters would shorten lives, the average span of life in the western provinces is now the best for all of Canada and one of the best in the world. As reported by the government, the baby boy born in the Canadian West has a life expectancy of 69.79 years and the baby girl, 75.66 years. The corresponding figures for the whole of Canada were given as 68.4 and 74.2 years respectively. It makes opinions expressed by the pessimists of pioneer years seem laughable. The editorial writer of 1881, for example, was warning that people "who are not frozen to death are maimed for life by frostbites."

After several months of winter, the coming of spring, with all its western warmth and cheer, is welcomed more than in those areas where cold weather is unknown. Moreover, western summers, without extreme heat or excessive rainfall, are among the finest, and autumn days, made distinctive by clear skies, harvest scenes in farm fields, and unbelievable colours in trees and shrubs, must be remembered for their beauty.

The area has the best sunshine record in Canada. When a city such as Edmonton reports an average of 2,212 hours of sunshine per year, it means the equivalent of six hours per day.

In any northern situation, winter days will be relatively short and summer days correspondingly long. Thus many hours of summer daylight make up for relatively short summer seasons, hastening plant growth and maturity and making it possible to grow useful crops in northern districts where the frost-free period is less than three months. The Medicine Hat district enjoys a long frost-free period, averaging 120 days or more, but farther north, and in some foothills' locations, the average may be less than 60 frost-free days.

Annual precipitation, including both rain and snow, may vary from an average of 11 or 12 inches in southwestern Saskatchewan and southeastern Alberta to a high of 94 inches at Prince Rupert. The parkland country which lies north of the prairies receives more precipitation than they do, the average for the prairie cities being approximately 16.5 inches. In most western districts, about one-third of the year's moisture comes from snow. Fortunately for farming people, however, about half of the year's moisture falls during the growing season: April, May, June, and July.

To a large extent, rainfall determines the type of agriculture which will be practised. Irrigation has made some growers less dependent upon rains, but most farmers continue to operate on a dry-land basis and know all about the hardships accompanying drought.

Captain John Palliser, whose survey reports were written just over a hundred years ago, placed most of southern Saskatchewan, the southwestern corner of Manitoba, and the southeastern corner of Alberta in his famous Palliser Triangle, marking these areas as extensions of the Great American Desert. Palliser considered these parts to be unsuited for cultivation; nevertheless, Palliser's fears were greatly exaggerated, and while a portion of the Triangle country should be kept for ranching, other parts will continue to be important producers of wheat and other crops.

Western people hear much discussion about their dry land, but it is a fact that much of the world's surface receives less moisture. About one-third of the planet's land is in arid zones, and there are places in the western United States where no precipitation whatever was recorded for several years at a time.

It is sometimes said that the Midwest gets its weather from the north and northwest. The prevailing winds are northwesterly, and during the winter they can be chilly indeed, but the Rocky Mountains have a moderating effect, and with the assistance of Pacific Ocean air currents, Alberta's winters are less severe than those in Saskatchewan and Manitoba. It is the province of British Columbia which has the mildest winters, however, and the temperature in the Vancouver-Victoria area rarely drops below zero.

People living near Canada's west coast enjoy a mild and distinctively agreeable climate, and for those living near the Rocky Mountains and foothills, there is the recurring winter joy of having low temperatures interrupted by warm southwesterly winds known as chinooks. Having their origin in the Pacific's warm Japanese current, these winds are capable of raising temperatures suddenly. People living at Pincher Creek, Fort Macleod, and points far north in the foothills can recall times when, after retiring at night with the temperature well below zero, they awakened the following morning to find the snow melting and water running.

Scientists have the best explanations for the behaviour of chinook winds, but Indians had the most attractive ones. According to campfire legend, a beautiful Indian girl known as Chinook wandered into the mountains and became lost. Gallant young braves searched diligently; however, they found no trace of the girl. They never saw her again, but when they felt warm breezes coming over the mountains from the southwest, they said: "Ah, it is the soft breath of our lost Chinook."

In spite of occasional complaints, midwestern weather is not characterized by extremes, either in winter or summer, yet there was Snag in the Yukon where the temperature on February 3, 1947, fell to 81° below zero. In looking for more extremes, it should be noted as well that at some points on the west coast of Vancouver Island the annual rainfall averages more than 100 inches.

Weather behaviour is far-reaching in its influence upon a country, affecting vegetation, landscape, industry, history, soil, and topography. As anybody who has travelled extensively knows, western scenes are varied and wonderful, ranging from plains to dense forests, from deep river valleys to mountain grandeur towering 12,000 feet above sea level, and from eroded badlands to icefields such as the Columbia on the Alberta-British Columbia border. Students and tourists alike have discovered the landscape wonders.

The midwestern portion of Canada, commonly called the prairies, is like a vast tableland, tilted to be higher on its Rocky Mountain side. Calgary, Canada's highest city, is at 3,545 feet above sea level, while Winnipeg's altitude is only 786 feet. It is easy to see why the general direction of riverflow is eastward and the three provinces share water from the Rocky Mountain watersheds.

Strangely enough, the run-off from Alberta does not go the same way. In fact, the province's streamwater contributes to oceans on three sides of the continent. Milk River in the south goes on to join the Missouri and Mississippi and, finally, the Gulf of Mexico; water from the North and

South Saskatchewan Rivers flows into Lake Winnipeg and then goes on to Hudson Bay; both the Peace and the Athabasca, big rivers cutting through the north, send their water to swell the mighty Mackenzie which in turn delivers to the Arctic Ocean. Although the region is fortunate in water resources, there is no reason to believe that Canadians in years to come will not need it all.

Of the many natural gifts inherited by western people, some were readily marketable. There were forests to support lumber and paper industries, minerals of many kinds inviting mining, coal in fabulous amounts, oil, gas, and so on. Of Canada's estimated 99 billion tons of mineable coal, it was found that Alberta had almost one-half, or 48 billion tons; Saskatchewan had 24 billion tons, and British Columbia had 19 billion tons.

Likewise, the largest proven reserves of oil and gas are in Alberta. Estimates in 1966 showed Canada's total reserves of natural gas to be 44.4 trillion cubic feet; of this total, Alberta had 36.4 trillion cubic feet, British Columbia had 6.8 trillion cubic feet, and Manitoba had about one trillion. The figures for crude oil gave Canada a total in proven reserves of 6.7 billion barrels, 95 per cent of which is to be found in Alberta, Saskatchewan, and Manitoba.

It should be noted that the figures for oil in reserve did not include the huge deposits in the McMurray sands where the petroleum wealth staggers the imagination. Estimates can be expected to vary, but there is reason to believe that those oil-soaked sands along the Athabasca River hold between 300 billion and 600 billion barrels of oil, making it the biggest known petroleum deposit in the entire world.

Nature seems to have tried to distribute the rich resources: British Columbia received the best in forests, Alberta inherited the biggest share of oil, natural gas, and coal, Manitoba received the prize of nickel, and Saskatchewan obtained the potash. Nickel production in Manitoba and Ontario placed Canada in a position of undisputed world leadership, while Saskatchewan's recently discovered potash has been described as the best of all potential aids in the struggle to relieve world hunger.

Rather suddenly, the people of Saskatchewan realized they had about half of all the known potash in the world, a legacy from an ancient and salty lake or sea which had evaporated, leaving a deep layer of potassium chloride extending from one side of Saskatchewan to the other, a distance of some 400 miles. Potash has various uses, but its main value is in meeting needs for crop fertilizer since it is one of the essential plant foods. Successful crop production on many of the world's soils depends upon its application.

Before the third Saskatchewan potash mine was in production, many more mines were in the planning stage, and western Canada was becoming recognized as the world's best source of the food-making fertilizer product. Coupled with other fertilizers being manufactured and wheat which prairie soil can supply, that potash made Canada a foremost country in furnishing relief from hunger. At 1965 rates of use, the potash under Saskatchewan could be sufficient to meet all world needs for the best part of a thousand years. Its discovery was another reason for western Canadians to pause and give thanks.

It is reassuring to count the many gifts in western Canada's treasure chest: wood, water, coal, iron, potash, sulphur, salt, wildlife, and soil. And the most precious of these is the one most commonly taken for granted, namely, soil, the source of most foods. Soil and climate explain much about the appearance of any countryside, and nobody really understands his province or his country until he has considerable knowledge of both.

Directly or indirectly, soil is basic to all human endeavour and should be considered in all public planning. Manitoba, Saskatchewan, and Alberta together have 75 per cent of the arable soils of Canada, but soils differ widely, just as the landscape on them differs widely. Why? Why are some soils more productive than others? Why does the mud near Winnipeg cling like glue to rubbers while at Carberry it does not behave that way? Why is soil brown at Medicine Hat, black at Edmonton, and grey at Athabasca? Every soil, by its character, expresses something of its origin, its parent material, the climate under which it was developed, and the kind of vegetation grown on it.

To explain differences in western soils, it is necessary to look into the distant past. The great ice masses which at one time or another covered the northern half of the continent, probably to a depth exceeding a thousand feet, made lasting impressions upon the country. As the ice from four or five ice ages advanced, it acted like a giant bulldozer, pushing and pulverizing stones, sand, and soil ahead of it, leaving exposed that big crescent-shaped belt of hard rock known as the Canadian Shield or Precambrian Shield. Then, when the climate changed enough to let the glaciers melt and retreat, they dropped their loads of stones and soil and left great amounts of water to form lakes or cut rivercourses. The glaciers clearly contributed a great deal in determining Canadian geography, accounting for ridges, valleys, lakes, riverbeds, sandhills, and much in soil character.

Naturally, a glacier would block any northward escape of water melting on its southern front, forcing the water to find an alternative place to go. With all the channels to the north blocked, water which might have followed the Saskatchewan River course flowed into a broad lake, such as the one covering Regina Plains at one period. From Lake Regina and Lake Rosetown, in country marked by today's Saskatchewan, water flowed into the Souris River and on to the Mississippi.

What is now Manitoba had some of the biggest glacial lakes: Lake Agassiz, covering over 100,000 square miles, Lake Brandon, and Lake Souris. Lake Agassiz is believed to have been 550 feet deep where the city of Winnipeg stands today. At that time its water drained southward; later, as glaciers retreated and lake levels dropped, the drainage was northward.

As its waters fell slowly, the old lake left successive sandy beaches, at least 27 of them, running parallel to the Pembina escarpment, southwest of Winnipeg. Ultimately, the disappearance of those glacial lakes left areas of deep lake silt which became the West's richest soils: those of Red River Valley, Regina Plains, and Rosetown Plains, southwest of Saskatoon. The action of glacial lake water also left the West with deposits of sand and sandy soils.

Soil surveys, which may have been the best of all public investments, began at the provincial universities in 1920 or soon after and, with provincial and federal government co-operation, continued without serious interruption.

Provincial soil maps show four, five, or six major zones. Starting in the driest part, there is the brown soil zone of southwestern Saskatchewan and southeastern Alberta, where precipitation is frequently less than 13 inches in a year. There, in an area of about 35,000,000 acres, with Medicine Hat at the centre, ranching is practised extensively.

Then, like a crescent-shaped band lying on the west, north, and east of the brown zone is the dark brown zone, not quite as dry. Like the brown zone, it is almost entirely in Alberta and Saskatchewan and contains the towns and cities of Lethbridge, Rosetown, Saskatoon, Regina, and Weyburn. The zone covers about 30,000,000 acres, and much of the West's best wheat has been grown in it.

Proceeding northward, the next in order is the black zone, sometimes divided into two zones or subzones. It is an area of roughly 42,000,000 acres with more rainfall and less evaporation. The term "Park Belt" comes from the presence of small groves of trees, mainly poplar and willow. The soil is comparatively rich in organic matter and nitrogen. Here are communities including Innisfail, Edmonton, Melfort, Moosomin, and Winnipeg.

Beyond the rich black soils are the grey wooded soils of Alberta and Saskatchewan and the high lime soils of Manitoba. Grey soils cover most of northern and northwestern Alberta. Some are quite low in fertility, but all support native vegetation, and many have fine stands of mixed forest trees.

What does it all mean? The history of a province or a nation will be shaped largely by the extent to which its people seize natural opportunities and exercise their own initiative. The fur traders and early travellers seemed blind to even the most obvious advantages, such as fertile soil, and there was no evidence of progress for many years. Since the years of fur trade, however, the inventory of known wealth in natural resources has grown rapidly and so has the number of people with ambition and vigour to use the resources. The result has been progress and prosperity.

But anyone who inherits something of great value also inherits the responsibility of understanding it and using it wisely. Only an ungrateful person would fail to understand and appreciate gifts. The citizen who acknowledges the country's favourable climate, the total absence of over-crowding which is a serious handicap in many parts of the world, and the opportunity of using and managing Nature's many contributions must conclude that there are few, if any, better and more challenging places to live.

It is good for people with pride in their surroundings to understand them more thoroughly, starting with the story of their development. Until people know what has gone before, they cannot assess the future accurately. In addition, the history of an area or a nation can be an absorbing study.

Dinosaur Bones Tell a Story

Western Canada's written history embraces little more than a couple of hundred years, but the fossilized bones of extinct animal species like the dinosaurs can tell a most remote past. The discovery of such bones along the Red Deer River, both upstream and downstream from Drumheller, has served to make Canadians very conscious of those fearsome creatures which inhabited these parts a hundred million years ago.

Primitive man hunted mastodons, mammoths, and sabre-toothed tigers, which are now also extinct, but dinosaurs and men never met. Those terrible lizards, as they have been called, flourished and then disappeared long before human beings came upon the scene. All that man was to see of them were the skeletons and parts of skeletons found in places like the Red Deer River Valley. There the bones, exposed by many centuries of erosion, can be seen as links with the surrounding countryside of millions of years ago.

Only by putting imaginary flesh on those old bones has it been possible to gain some knowledge of the physical appearance of dinosaurs. They came in many shapes and sizes and were widely distributed, so that no single area had exclusive claim to them. Recent reports told of skeletons of an ostrich-like dinosaur, similar to specimens found in Alberta, being dug up in the Gobi Desert of Asia. At about the same time, a previously unknown form was uncovered in Wyoming, this one being a carnivorous species, no bigger than a Collie dog and thought to have lived 130 million years ago.

Although no area had any monopoly in the matter of dinosaur remains, the Red Deer River Valley became the best-known source of specimens for museum purposes. Western Canadians visiting museums in far parts of the world have found themselves facing dinosaur skeletons reconstructed from bones discovered in the Red Deer River Badlands.

Dr. J. B. Tyrrell, Dominion Government geologist, visited the Red Deer River in 1884 and may have been the first to take dinosaur bones for museum displays. Almost at once, scientists from many parts of the world were attracted. In 1909, Barnum Brown of New York made a special trip to Steveville and other places on the river, recovering a skeleton which was taken to New York. Since that time, the valley of the Red Deer has gained recognition as the world's most fruitful source of dinosaur skeletons and at least 40 scientific expeditions have been made to it.

The most intensive work of discovery and recovery was conducted by members of the Sternberg family. In 1912, Charles M. Sternberg, who became a paleontologist of world renown, discovered the complete skeleton of a dinosaur belonging to the duckbill species, which was fond of swimming. This can still be seen at the National Museum in Ottawa. Another duckbill was reconstructed and given a place of prominence at St. George's Island Park in Calgary.

It must be presumed that much of this wheat and cattle country in which bones have been discovered was once the floor of a shallow and steamy sea extending from the Gulf of Mexico to the Arctic. This was an area supporting tropical plants, giant sequoia and redwood trees, cinnamon and fig trees, and reptiles of many kinds.

There can be no doubt about the shape and size of the dinosaurs thanks to the fossilized evidence which has been found. Some of the creatures were small, like present-day lizards; some were huge, like the "Dinny" model in Calgary's St. George's Park. The biggest of the dinosaurs, Brontosaurus or "thunder lizard," about 90 feet long and 30 feet high, has not been uncovered in the Red Deer Valley, that is, not yet. Nevertheless, of the 30 distinct species identified there, many were big indeed.

Some of the biggest were vegetarians; others, like the 40-foot Gorgosaurus, were meat eaters. Some were duckbills and liked to swim in the brackish water, preferring the marshy deltas near Drumheller; others lived on high ground. Some had hard and tough exteriors, a sort of armour-plated protection; others had horns. All were probably ugly in appearance.

At death, many of those marshland inhabitants sank into the mud, where their bones became petrified and remained hidden for millions of years before they were exposed by the erosive forces of wind and water.

E. W. Cadman, Calgary

"Dinny" is a Brontosaurus who lived over 130 million years ago. He had a deep, massive body, a long neck, and a tail which ended in a whiplash tip. His legs formed thick columns ending in feet which were as much as 26 inches wide and thought to be padded like those of the elephant. The fully developed toes bore claws: one on each forefoot and three massive claws behind. In natural life he may have weighed as much as 65 tons.

It does not mean that all the dinosaurs chose the Red Deer River country as a place to live and die; probably many other parts of Alberta and the land beyond became hiding places for the mineralized remains in equal abundance, but only in the Red Deer Valley did the forces of erosion do such a thorough job in laying them bare.

Because of the damage erosion is capable of doing to agricultural lands, it is regarded as a serious enemy but, in the case of the Red Deer Valley, the action not only exposed useful information about the area's remote past, but left the fascinating Badlands whose landscape led to the establishment of a most distinctive provincial park. The shapes cut in clay, shale, and sandstone are weird and eerie: cones, hoodoos, needles, and buttes, making the whole valley look like a playground for ghosts and witches. Long ago, the landscape became a delight to artists and camera fans, and a source of amazement to tourists, but nothing in the valley grips the imagination as much as the realization that the slow processes of erosion, while carving a prairie wonderland, laid bare many of the continent's secrets of the ages.

For many visitors, the urge to gather specimens is very strong, and tons of dinosaur bones have been trucked away by trophy-hunters, some of them not really knowing what they had. It would be better if these age-old treasures were recovered only by trained people or under proper supervision, and with all the care science can provide.

The recovery of dinosaur bones, or any old bones, by technical workers is a slow and tedious undertaking. If this process were carried out with more haste and less painstaking care, the bones would be likely to disintegrate and lose their character and value. The scientists' method involves, first of all, the careful removal of the clay or other surrounding material by hand. Then the bones are treated with shellac and finally placed in plaster of paris casts before being moved for shipment. A casual observer at a museum in which a Red Deer Valley skeleton is on display is not likely to consider the tremendous amount of patient work involved in removing the bones from their ancient beds and piecing them together for public inspection.

Any dinosaur bones tell a gripping story. It is the story of an era long before the appearance of mammals, long before the glaciers moved far across the face of this country, long before the climate took on its present characteristics, even before the Rocky Mountains broke the horizon. Even a mental picture of the prairie country as a tropical everglade, overrun with wicked-looking lizard monsters, is not easy to grasp. It was a strange community.

But gradually it changed. The mountains towered skyward and other continental shifts occurred; the water in the warm inland sea drained away. Animals of all kinds were obliged to make major adjustments or give up. The big dinosaurs, the mightiest living things the world has known, might have seemed like crowning biological achievements, but their bulky and imposing forms did nothing to ensure survival. In the course of time, they too, like certain other animal species, disappeared completely. Nobody knows the exact reason, but one may speculate about a disappearance which followed a change in environment to which the animals failed to adjust.

This carries with it the reminder that no race or species, no matter how big or fast or fierce or smart, has any guarantee of surviving forever. Much depends upon the race's strength and its ability to maintain a continuing state of harmony with its natural surroundings. The living things which become strangers in Nature's community are in serious danger of weakening their grip upon the future. But with the disappearance of dinosaurs, some new species of animals appeared. Some of them, like horses, are well known to modern people.

One talks about this being a young country. It is true that the written record is short, but the record captured by the rocks and old bones is one to fire the imagination.

Early Man on Western Soil

The white man has made many mistakes in his hasty judgements of native people: his first was in calling them Indians. Columbus, sailing westward in 1492, expected to reach China, and when he touched the Caribbean Islands, he took them to be the Indies which lie off the coast of Asia. If these were the Indies, it seemed logical to call the inhabitants Indians. The name has remained.

Nobody knows exactly the size of native population at the time of Columbus, perhaps a few million on the continent, of which perhaps a quarter of a million lived in what was to become Canada. But since when had the race been here and from where did its first members come?

Indians chose to believe their ancestors were created on this soil, but the best evidence points to a different explanation. Until recent discoveries near Medicine Hat, there was no indication of human occupation prior to the Ice Age, leading to the conclusion that the earliest immigrants came within the last 25,000 years. But artifacts found together with fossilized mammoth and camel bones in southeastern Alberta are believed to be 30,000 years old.

Nobody can rule out the possibility of pioneer adventurers drifting eastward across the South Pacific or westward across the South Atlantic to establish their race in the Americas, but it is more likely that the Indians' ancestors came from Asia by way of the Bering Strait, at a time when the two continents were connected by a land bridge.

Even today, the distance between the northeastern point of Asia and the western tip of Alaska is only about 50 miles. In glacial ages, when much of the world's water was piled up as ice on northern land masses, ocean levels may have been low enough to make for a land connection between the two continents. It could have been the principal route over which human beings reached North America, as well as the route by which wild animals, such as mammoths, horses, and camels, travelled from one continent to the other.

It is easy to imagine human newcomers making their way southward by way of the Mackenzie River Valley, lured by better hunting than they had seen before. As their numbers increased, they fanned out to occupy distant parts of the continent, forming different clans and tribes. Living with friends and relations, in groups or tribes, had many advantages. It offered companionship and, best of all, a chance of putting up a strong fight in case of an enemy attack. The discovery of ancient burial places, campfire sites, bone piles, and stone implements has helped to show where the newcomers went and how they lived.

By the time Jacques Cartier came to the St. Lawrence River, the division into tribes was clear. The eastern section of the country had its Beothuk Indians in Newfoundland, Micmacs in Nova Scotia territory, Montagnais north of the St. Lawrence, and Algonquin, Iroquois, Mohawk, Huron, Tobacco, and Ojibway farther inland. British Columbia had numerous small tribes: Kootenay, Salish, Chilcotin, Bella Coola, Nootka, Haida, and others. The prairies had a few big and powerful ones: the Assiniboines representing a break-away branch of the more southerly Sioux, the Crees who might be either Wood Crees or Plains Crees, the Sarcees who were related to the Chipewyans of the North, the Stonies who liked to think of themselves as Mountain Sioux, and the three member-tribes of the Black-foot Confederacy; namely, Blackfoot, Bloods, and Piegans. Chipewyans, Slaves, and Beavers were in the country lying north of the prairies.

Language differed considerably, with Stonies and Assiniboines speaking in the Siouan tongue, Sarcees speaking Athabaskan, Crees and members of the Blackfoot group speaking Algonkian. On the west coast, at least four distinct languages were spoken by the local tribes.

Although they fought almost perpetually, Indians of the prairie tribes differed very little in either their habits or appearance. They were of medium height and generally lean; they had copper-coloured skins, straight, black hair, and brown eyes.

When white men met them, they were still very much in the Stone Age, employing knowledge about chipping flint which their ancestors brought from Asia. Bows and arrows were their principal hunting weapons, but they found use for tomahawks, hammers, and spears, all made from native stone. Their finest skill was expressed in shaping arrowheads and fitting them to willow or cherrywood shafts. Even after the introduction of guns, many Indians continued to use bows and arrows because such weapons allowed for noiseless hunting and, sometimes, more slaughter.

People who like to tramp over prairie fields today know the thrill of finding arrowheads, some of them thousands of years old and delicately shaped and beautiful. Archaeology, the study of early human activities as revealed by surviving relics, is a fascinating interest at any time, and even in the Alberta countryside the opportunities for pursuing it are rich.

Flint was a favourite material for making arrowheads, but when it was not available, many other kinds of stones were used. It is noteworthy that of the thousands of arrowheads found in western soil no two are exactly alike in colour, size, shape, and workmanship. They range from small points of half an inch in length to those of six inches in length. The biggest ones might be more accurately classified as spearheads.

Most arrowheads were fashioned with notches which made it possible to lash them securely to arrow shafts, but some were without notches, and certain specimens called Folsom points have been given special attention. Scientists working near the town of Folsom in New Mexico found specimens of this rather unusual type in association with bones of a long-extinct species of North American buffalo. The discovery made them wonder if it might indicate that the Indian race had been on this continent longer than they had previously thought probable.

Some archaeologists suggested a special purpose for those arrowheads without the usual notches. They could have had an advantage in war. The common type of arrowhead with notches to make it secure on the shaft could be removed from the body of a game animal or the body of an enemy tribesman by pulling on the shaft. In this way the arrowhead could be used again, and the wounded enemy would have a better chance of recovery if the entire arrow were removed. For the same reason, a point of the Folsom type could be more deadly in battle and might have been favoured by warriors. A wounded brave might attempt to pull out the

Because they were nomads, the Indians of the prairies lived in homes which were easily set up and dismantled. The homes seen here, or "tipis", as the Indians called them, are near the Elbow of the Saskatchewan River.

Public Archives of Canada

embedded arrow, only to find that he had removed the shaft and left the Folsom arrowhead deep in his body.

Unfortunately, present-day Indians know nothing about the art of flaking flint and shaping arrowheads. They can make pipes from soapstone or pipestone but nothing more.

Differing from eastern tribes, the prairie Indians lived almost exclusively by hunting. Iroquois and Hurons carried on a form of agriculture, growing corn, beans, and tobacco, and members of the Ojibway and Assiniboine tribes gathered wild rice. But in buffalo country, the diet consisted almost entirely of buffalo meat. After the allotment of reserves in southern Alberta, the hungry Indians acted as though they had been insulted when government officers offered them flour. They wanted meat, particularly buffalo meat. Every adult male Indian was a buffalo hunter, skilled in shooting from the back of a horse at full gallop, skilled in mass killing by stampeding a herd over a cutbank.

All the Canadian tribes were more or less nomadic, that is, they had no permanent homes, but these buffalo-hunting Indians of the prairies wandered more than those of any other group on the continent. Being tipi-dwellers, moving was simple, and Indians generally tried to stay within striking distance of the herds. Moreover, it was a mistake in a warlike community to remain long in one place.

Hunting methods changed somewhat when the Indians obtained horses and changed still more when guns came into their hands. They quickly became expert horsemen; however, they never domesticated any of the native animals although they had dogs which probably could be traced to stock brought from Asia. The horses they ultimately rode were from stock introduced by Spaniards who followed Columbus to the New World.

Nothing changed the lives of the Indians as much as the ownership of horses. Surely these animals were the white man's finest contribution to them, partly making up for the evils of whisky and disease.

Indians of the far south were the first to obtain and ride horses. The new horse owners immediately became more effective in the hunt and more successful in battle. When one tribe had horses, it seemed essential for neighbouring tribesmen to get them, and the great Indian sport of horse stealing was started. Having never thought of stealing as being wrong, men of every tribe wanted to be experts.

The first of the new horse stock seen in what is now Alberta was being ridden by Snake Indians in the Bow River area about 1730. Horses gave the Snakes a big advantage, and their enemies felt the need to obtain them by any possible means. Consequently, the Blackfoot stole horses from the Snakes; then the Crees stole from the Blackfoot, and the Assiniboines stole wherever they saw the opportunity. Very soon, prairie Indians of all tribes were mounted and enjoying the big changes in their ways of living. They became clever horsemen, clever in shooting from their horses' backs, clever in creeping into an enemy encampment and making off with the best horses.

But life for the Indians was to change greatly. It was a shock for these "rulers of the plains" to be forced to surrender their freedom and live on reservations. The last of the major Indian treaties, Blackfoot Treaty Number Seven, was signed at Blackfoot Crossing on the Bow River late in 1877. Although the Blackfoot, Blood, Piegan, Sarcee, and Stoney Indians accepted reservation life, they hated it and longed for the old days when they were free to pitch tipis anywhere and ride out after game without worrying about reservation boundaries. They found it difficult to forgive the white man for seizing their lands, and the thought of rebellion and massacre often flashed through their minds.

The white man's numbers and strength in weapons were too much for Indians, however, and life on the reservations went on with very little change. Many Canadian leaders wanted to do something to improve the Indians' status, but it was difficult to know what to do. Some people believed the best hope was to integrate the Indians with the white race, eventually doing away with the reservations and the segregated life they represented. Others, fearful that integration would mean the ultimate disappearance of the smaller race, believed Indians were entitled to every chance to remain as Indians and live like Indians. The reservations, or something like them, seemed to offer the best chance for Indians to preserve their identity.

White men who deprived them of their land, destroyed the herds supplying their food, and uprooted them from their religion and freedom and way of life failed to recognize many of their fine and noble characteristics. There were many great thinkers among them, men like Chief Crowfoot whose oratory and reasoning should have made him admired by men of all races. He contended that his Indian people had ideals which should not be allowed to become lost. In answer to any thought of allowing the white race to absorb Indians, he would have joined with another great thinker, Walking Buffalo, in saying: "The Great Spirit created Indians to be Indians. Don't try to make white men of them. Better a good Indian than a poor white man."

The Wild Herds

At the time of the white man's coming, prairie Indians depended upon the buffalo for nearly all their needs. They ate fresh buffalo meat as long as they could get it, and when they could not get it because the herds were far away, they ate pemmican which they made from a mixture of dried buffalo meat and saskatoon berries. From buffalo skins they made articles of clothing, covers for tipis, and robes to serve as blankets for their beds. A stomach removed from the body of a dead buffalo could be used as a handy basket or container for carrying food and water; buffalo bones could be fashioned into knives and other tools. It was not surprising that Indians occupying the prairie areas thought of those big animals as special gifts to them from the Great Spirit.

The buffalo were picturesque, about the size and weight of domestic cattle, but heavier in the fore quarters and lighter in the hind. Thanks to their sharp horns and powerful bodies, they were strong fighters and generally managed to survive to the age of ten or twelve years.

What is now southern Alberta and southern Saskatchewan may have been the best of all buffalo country. The grass was short but nutritious, and it furnished good feed in winter as well as summer. It brought an advantage to the Blackfoot Indians living in that part and, knowing their good fortune in being so favourably located, they fought savagely to protect their good hunting ground.

But the buffalo herds did not stay in one place. Actually, they roamed far, and stragglers might have been seen as far north as Lesser Slave Lake. Some of the animals, undoubtedly, wintered in the Park Belt; however, there is reason to believe that the largest numbers remained on the southern prairies and migrated northward in the spring.

It was at a time of migration that the animals came together to form the biggest herds, giving the impression that the plains were black with buffaloes. A Northwest Mounted Police officer riding from Fort Macleod to Fort Qu'Appelle told that for days he was never out of sight of the buffalo. And Rev. John McDougall, the pioneer Methodist missionary, told of standing on Spy Hill, on Calgary's north side, and seeing buffalo herds on all sides. He believed he was seeing fully half a million of the big animals at that time.

For most of any year, Indians had no trouble in killing enough buffalo to meet all food needs, and they tried to move often enough to be always near fresh supplies. Sometimes the animals were far away and it was then that the native people drew upon their reserves of pemmican; however, when they could, they killed freely, often recklessly, and took only the choicest parts of the carcasses: the humps and tongues. They loved the buffalo hunt, especially after they got horses, and every hunt was a wild and exciting chase. The Assiniboine Indians were particularly successful in constructing pounds or big corrals into which the buffalo might be chased or lured for the killing, and all the prairie tribesmen occasionally resorted to slaughter by stampeding a herd over a steep cutbank.

No doubt there was waste as well as cruelty, but the herds were huge and Indian killing made no permanent difference to the total buffalo numbers. It was only after the white man came and found interest in selling buffalo hides that the herds began to shrink and then to disappear. The destruction of the mighty herds in a brief period of ten years makes one of the sad chapters in Canadian history. When the Northwest Mounted Police made their long journey westward to build Fort Macleod in 1874, the wild things must have numbered many millions; by 1884, the wild herd was practically gone.

How could the sudden, even shocking, disappearance be explained? Disease has been suggested as a possible reason for the tragedy, but members of the buffalo race had always been healthy and quite free from disease. Did a particularly severe winter destroy a big percentage of the animals? That, too, seems unlikely because the buffalo was extremely hardy and well protected against cold weather. The coat of hair was thick and, over the head and shoulders, it was especially long. Men have found that buffalo hide coats afford the very best of outdoor protection against winter winds and frost. While a domestic cow would turn her back to a storm, the buffalo turned head to the wind and did not seem to hesitate about travelling against it.

Nor was it likely that natural enemies accounted for the sudden disappearance. Wolves might kill an occasional buffalo calf, but the adult buffalo had no reason to fear attack from any wild animals. The grown buffalo bull was a hard fighter and could probably hold his own against even a grizzly bear.

Everything points to the hide-hunters, equipped with new guns, as the chief offenders in the rapid destruction. Eastern leather manufacturers wanted buffalo hides. A successful hunter expected to kill 2,000 of the animals in a season and with hides selling for $2.00 each, the reward seemed attractive.

Buffalo Bill Cody, working on the south side of the international boundary, killed 4,280 in a period of 18 months. And J. A. Gaff, who ranched in southwestern Saskatchewan for about 40 years, claimed a bigger record: 5,200 in his best season, when hunting in Kansas during the seventies. Many thousands of hides were sent from Fort Calgary and Fort Macleod to Fort Benton in Montana. Some were collected at Fort Edmonton, Fort Pitt, Fort Carlton, and other Saskatchewan River posts and freighted to Winnipeg. Shipments eastward from the western states ran to millions. The I. G. Baker Company alone was known to have shipped 250,000 hides from Fort Benton in the single season of 1874, sending most of them by riverboat to New Orleans. At the same time, it may have been United

Photo Gano

This buffalo bull was photographed in Wainwright Park, Alberta, which for many years held the biggest surviving herd in the world.

States policy to hasten the killing of buffalo as a means of inducing Indians to settle on reservations.

When the herds were already seriously depleted, some attempts were made to protect the animals remaining. At the first meeting of the Council of the North West Territories, held in 1877 at Livingstone, beside the Swan River, an order was passed for the protection of the buffalo, but it was either ineffective or too late. After another two or three years, hungry Indians searched in vain. In a surprisingly short time, the destruction of the wild herd was complete. Only white bones scattered across the prairies remained to tell of the big bands of previous years.

But the bones were not wasted. In fact, they represented the first products many homesteaders had to sell and the first cargo to be shipped out of the country after the Canadian Pacific Railway was built across the Territories.

Bones gathered and delivered at new shipping points and selling for $5.00 and $6.00 per ton at country stations helped new settlers to pay for groceries and supplies until their first grain crop was ready for market. Railway sidings between Regina and Calgary saw thousands of tons of the bones loaded on freight cars and shipped to Chicago or St. Paul for use in bleaching sugar or making fertilizer. New branch lines also carried heavy shipments of the bones, and Saskatoon alone was known to have accounted for more than 3,000 carloads.

Fortunately, a few of the magnificent buffaloes did survive in parks and on privately owned ranges. By the year 1907, the biggest remaining herd on the continent consisted of a few hundred animals owned by Michael Pablo of Montana. Faced with the loss of his government range, Pablo had to sell. The government of the United States refused to buy and Norman Luxton of Banff, hearing about it, suggested to Sir Wilfrid Laurier that Canada make the purchase. Negotiations were successful, and Ottawa authorities instructed that the herd of some 716 animals bought for $245 per head be moved to Canadian parks.

To round up and ship the wild animals was a most difficult task, but the best of cowboys were obtained for the work and it was carried out quite expertly. The first two shipments were to Elk Island Park, east of Edmonton, and the balance of the herd, 631 head, was sent to the bigger park range at Wainwright.

It seemed most appropriate that Canada should now have the biggest remaining herd of buffaloes. According to legend, the Pablo herd traced entirely to stock which had gone to the United States from Canada. A Pend d'Oreille Indian had come to the Canadian side to get away from an overbearing mother-in-law, but after being away for a couple of years, he became lonely and decided to return to Montana. Thinking it might be wise to take a gift for his mother-in-law, he captured four buffalo calves in the southern part of the prairies and drove them to the Mission of St. Ignatius in Montana. Perhaps the orphan calves followed him. In any case, he managed to deliver them and present them in the hope they would win the mother-in-law's good will. There is no information about the young fellow's success in buying favour, but the animals grew and became the foundation for the big privately-owned herd which was to come into Canadian ownership.

The buffalo herds increased in numbers at both Canadian parks, and surplus animals were sent from Wainwright to Wood Buffalo Park on Alberta's northern boundary. By 1935, Canada had 17,000 of the animals, mainly in three parks: Wainwright, Elk Island, and Wood Buffalo, but in 1939, at the beginning of World War II, the Government of Canada ordered the clearing of Wainwright Park for use in the new military program. The buffalo herd was again the victim of man's erratic schemes. Some were moved to Wood Buffalo Park and the remainder destroyed.

Nevertheless, Canadians lost none of their interest in the big herds remaining at Elk Island and Wood Buffalo Parks. Because of the locations of these parks, prairie people had a special interest and invited their tourist

A skull lying on the plains which were once inhabited solely by buffalo, a sad reminder of the proud animal almost completely destroyed by the white man's greed.

Ashdown Johnson

visitors to inspect them. From the point of view of western Canadian history, however, the most important events in the buffalo chapter, both good and bad, came in the few years after 1874 when the wild herds were killed off and the country cleared for other uses like ranching, homesteading, and the building of villages, towns, and cities.

2 Furs — The West's First Industry

The Years of the Fur Trade

Wild furs were the first of Canadian resources to receive the white man's attention, and for more than two centuries there was practically no other reason for coming to the new land. Although this constituted an exciting chapter in Canadian history, it was not a glorious one in all respects if one considers the ruthless killing involved and the thoughtless use of steel traps.

The approach to the fur country from the East was by way of the St. Lawrence River, up which Jacques Cartier sailed on his second voyage to the continent in 1535; in the West, it was by way of Hudson Bay, described as the Great Bay of the North. A glance at the map will show how the deep bay made it possible for ocean-going ships to penetrate far into the western country, long called Rupert's Land.

The great bay took its name from Henry Hudson who was the first European to see it. In 1610, he set sail under a British flag. His aim was to look for China and he hoped, at least, to find a route through northern waters to that eastern country. Poor Hudson never did see China; indeed, he never again saw his homeland because members of his crew became alarmed by the bleak Eskimo country they saw, and when Hudson refused to turn back, they mutinied. Feeling desperate, they cast their captain adrift in a small boat on the cold water of the bay and sailed toward home with cowardly haste.

Other explorers came to search for Hudson, but he was never seen again. As the years passed, however, French fur traders travelled farther and farther inland from Montreal. Two of the best known, Radisson and

Groseilliers, ventured as far as Lake Superior and north from there, finding the beaver skins in northern districts to have thicker and finer fur than any they had seen before. They heard about the salt sea somewhere north of Lake Superior and wondered if it might be possible for French traders to reach Indians in that remote part by ship.

When they returned to the city of Quebec in 1663, the two adventuresome explorers had 300 canoes loaded with fine northern furs to show for their absence. But because they had been travelling and exploring without the French governor's permission, they were arrested and fined and had their furs taken from them.

Failing to obtain aid or encouragement from the governor of French Canada, they turned to France and then to England where they were well received by Prince Rupert, cousin of King Charles II. As a result of the stories told by these two daring Frenchmen who were nicknamed "Radish and Gooseberry", an expedition backed by Charles II of England, Prince Rupert, and a number of London businessmen, was sent to Hudson Bay in 1668. One of the two ships had trouble and was obliged to turn back, but the other, called *The Nonsuch*, made a successful journey and returned the next year, loaded with the best furs English merchants had seen. Londoners were eager to get more furs like them and, in 1670, King Charles granted a charter to a company described as "The Governor and Company of Adventurers of England Trading into Hudson's Bay." It marked the beginning of the Hudson's Bay Company, "the true and absolute Lordes and Proprietors", existing today as the only concern with an unbroken record of almost 300 years of business in Canada.

The first governor of the Company was Prince Rupert, an extremely favourable arrangement. What more could be desired than to have all trading privileges in the big country where stream water drained toward Hudson Bay? The area included all of the present provinces of Manitoba and Saskatchewan, much of southern Alberta, and parts of northern Ontario, Quebec, the Northwest Territories, and the states of Minnesota and North Dakota.

In this big portion of the continent, the Company would have the right to govern, to make and enforce laws. In return, the English king or his heir could expect to collect two black elk skins and two black beaver skins at any time the royal guest went into the country.

At first, the Company traders were satisfied to remain at their posts on the coast: Fort Charles, Fort Nelson, Moose Factory, Fort Albany, Fort Churchill, and so on, and let the Indians bring furs to them. With a good fort on the coast of the bay, Company men felt sure that they could protect their big fur empire. It was with this in mind that the Company built Fort Churchill and then the massive Fort Prince of Wales on the west coast of

Hudson Bay. It was quite evident that the French would try to drive the English from the bay, as they had tried before, and the site at the mouth of the Churchill River appeared as the best place from which to defend the farflung Rupert's Land.

Fort Churchill was built in 1718 but was destroyed by fire soon after. It was then that plans were made for the mightiest fortification of all, Fort Prince of Wales, its great stone walls still standing like a dedication to eternity. Plans were drawn by military engineers, and construction began in 1732. How the huge boulders were skidded into place in the walls at a time when mechanical aids were unknown must remain a mystery.

The fort's dimensions are impressive. At its outer corners, it stands 300 feet by 300 feet. The thickness of the walls at the base ranges from 30 feet in the back wall to 42 feet in the front wall which carried most of the cannons.

Started in 1732, Fort Prince of Wales was finished 39 years later but, strange to relate, the massive structure was lost to the French without the firing of a shot from any of the 42 heavy cannons on the walls. Having sailed into Hudson Bay with only three ships, La Pérouse, the French admiral, was surprised to win the prize of war so easily. His main interest was in destroying the fort; however, as he discovered, the great stone structure was extremely difficult to destroy and little damage was inflicted upon it.

Very wisely, the Government of Canada has taken steps in recent years to see that the old fort is preserved as one of the nation's finest relics of history. More Canadians should see that memorial of the fur trade, the oldest man-made structure in the entire West.

It was all very well for English traders to sit beside the bay and wait for Indians to come with their furs. It worked for a while, but then tireless men from Montreal began travelling far inland to secure the furs. Company men saw how they were losing business and knew they had to start going to the Indians instead of waiting for the Indians to come to the bay. Henry Kelsey was the first to travel far inland from the Company's posts. In 1691, he was tramping over country which is now known as northern Saskatchewan and was surprised at the big buffalo herds he saw. With Indians as his teachers, young Kelsey was a good pupil, living and hunting like an Indian for most of a year. He returned to the bay with friendly Crees and a big cargo of furs.

Then, from Montreal, came Sieur de la Vérendrye and his sons. Their motives of exploration, the search for a route to the western sea and China and furs, were familiar. From Lake Superior westward they built trading posts: Fort St. Pierre on Rainy Lake, Fort St. Charles on Lake of the Woods, Fort Maurepas near the mouth of Winnipeg River, Fort Rouge where the Assiniboine joins the Red, Fort la Reine close to the present city of Portage la Prairie, and Fort Dauphin on the west side of Lake Manitoba.

After building Fort La Reine in 1738, la Vérendrye set out in a southwesterly direction, on an expedition which took him to the Mandan Indians in the Missouri River area. To his bitter disappointment, however, the natives in that part could give him no information about a water route to the western sea.

When the elder la Vérendrye was obliged to return to Montreal, he left his son Louis-Joseph, better known as Chevalier, in charge of the western posts. In the spring of 1749, Louis-Joseph paddled west on the river he called Pascoyac, later the Saskatchewan, quite sure he was at last on a water course to the western sea and China. Along the way, he chose a good place for a post which would effectively intercept many Indians taking furs to Hudson Bay. His name for the location was Pascoyac; to later Canadians it was The Pas, Manitoba.

Young la Vérendrye continued westward to the forks of the North and South Saskatchewan Rivers, still convinced he had found the coveted route to the western sea. It was a route he intended to pursue with his father in another year, but the father died soon after, and the son was unable to return.

A few years later, Chevalier de la Corne paddled to a point near the forks and built a post north of where the town of Kinistino, Saskatchewan, later emerged. This post, which carried its founder's name, was one more obstacle to the movement of Indian-owned furs to the bay, one more reason why the Hudson's Bay Company had to do something to meet the rising competition.

It fell to the lot of a young fellow in the Company's service at York Factory, Anthony Henday, to embark upon the most notable adventure of all. Henday's home was the Isle of Wight and if he had a profession there, it was that of smuggling. When he was outlawed because of his illegal conduct, he sailed for Hudson Bay to begin a new life. Lacking nothing in courage, he was ready for an adventure into the unknown Indian country, and on June 26, 1754, he and some Indians left York Factory. His Indian companions knew the water course well, and they took Henday to the Saskatchewan River. There he stopped to visit the Frenchman in charge of Fort Pascoyac where he received a not altogether cordial welcome. When the French trader heard of Henday's reasons for the trip, he considered making the man a prisoner and sending him to France to face charges of intruding upon French trade. Henday showed no fear, and even said he believed he could enjoy a trip to France. In the end, however, Henday was presenting the Frenchman with two feet of Brazile tobacco and leaving on good terms.

Further upstream, Henday's Indians chose to abandon their canoes and travel overland in the hope of meeting up with their own people. Henday, who was living like an Indian, had no objections, and the party set off on foot. Sure enough, the Indians did locate their families.

After a halt for reunion and celebration, members of the travelling party were on their way again, and three and one-half months after leaving the bay, Henday was visiting with Blood Indians in what is now central Alberta, perhaps between Red Deer River and today's town of Innisfail. Henday was the first white man these Indians had seen, and they gazed at him with astonishment. He was able to win their friendship, and he spent the winter with them, but he was unable to convince them to take their furs over the long route to Hudson Bay. The Bloods, like the Blackfoot, were not familiar with canoes, and the Indian chief could think of still other reasons for refusing to go. The distance was long, his people liked buffalo meat better than any other food, and they would be unwilling to travel far from buffalo country. Anyway, as the chief concluded, the Indians would not be any better off by trading at the bay.

Henday admitted the chief's reasoning was right. The Indians had plenty to eat, they needed no clothing, and they were contented. Would they be any happier with an introduction to the white man's business world? Toward spring, Henday started on the long return to his home base on Hudson Bay, taking with him many canoes loaded with furs. His mistake was in stopping at la Corne's fort and then Pascoyac, at both of which there was French brandy. The result was that Henday's Indians were easily persuaded to part with many of their best furs and the value of the cargo destined for the Company was seriously reduced. In due course, however, Henday was back at York Factory, trying to convince the officers there that he really did see snow-capped mountains and Indians riding horses.

The Battle of the Plains of Abraham beside the city of Quebec in 1759, just four years after Henday's notable adventure, seemed to change the course of history for a big part of the continent. For the Hudson's Bay Company, there would be no more of the prolonged and recurring conflict with the French on Hudson Bay; and, in the inland fur trade, most of the ensuing competition was to come from Montreal men with Scottish names.

The competition was in no way less vigorous, however, and Company men realized they must meet the Indians in their own territory. In 1774, Samuel Hearne built a Hudson's Bay Company post, Cumberland House, on the Saskatchewan River. It was the first clear demonstration of change in Company policy.

Now the competition to get furs was keener than ever. The Montreal men, "pedlars" as Hudson's Bay people called them, were extremely aggressive and did not hesitate to use rum in dealing with the Indians. They were fanning out into new country, defying the Royal Charter granted to the Company. One of their number, Peter Pond, was the first to build a post, Pond's House, in what is now Alberta. He continued northward via the Methye Portage and pioneered the Athabasca area. It was the richest fur country in the entire West. That was in 1778. In his first year there, he obtained twice as many furs as he was able to take out with the canoes available. Pond was quite a man, and not always on good behaviour. Twice he was under suspicion in connection with deaths by shooting in the Athabasca area. On both occasions he was acquitted by Montreal courts. Nevertheless, he was a fearless adventurer, and to add to many distinctions, Pond was the first to cultivate ground and plant garden seeds within the bounds of present-day Alberta.

Not long after the foundation of Pond's House, another post was erected a few miles away from it, on the shore of Lake Athabasca. This post was called Fort Chipewyan, and for a long time it was known as the Emporium of the North.

As the fur trade was extended westward, the men from Montreal faced higher transportation costs and decided to work together. In 1787, they formed the North West Company, with such names in the trade as Simon Fraser, Joseph Frobisher, Simon McTavish, James McGill, Peter Pond, and Alexander Mackenzie, giving it somewhat the aura of the membership list of a Scottish society. Nevertheless, the new partners were determined to go after furs with more fighting determination than ever. Man for man, the North Westers could generally surpass the Hudson's Bay people of that time, whether in canoes, on snowshoes, or in driving bargains with Indians. The English company's problem was to hold its own against the more ruthless Canadians or pedlars.

A canoe journey between Montreal and Athabasca took nearly four months. Such a long haul for freight was a huge handicap, but the North West Company men built lavishly at Grand Portage, on the west side of Lake Superior, naming the post "Half Way House". Grand Portage saw stirring times, especially when partners from Montreal met partners from the far West for annual meetings.

There, at Grand Portage, almost at the present international boundary, the 35-foot-long Montreal canoes with paddling crews of 10 or 12 men, and loaded with trade goods from the East, met and exchanged cargoes with the 25-foot North canoes, handled by 6 or 8 men and loaded with bales of furs. There the pork-eaters from the St. Lawrence and the pemmican-eaters from the West rested and celebrated before embarking upon the return journey; there the proud Montreal officials met the weather-beaten traders and clerks from posts as far away as Athabasca and discussed policies and plans for the seasons ahead.

The best fur harvest was still far to the north and west. The Montreal company built Fort George on the North Saskatchewan, about 40 miles west of the present Alberta-Saskatchewan boundary. The Hudson's Bay Company followed suit and built Buckingham House just across the river. It was the first Hudson's Bay Company post west of what is now the province of Saskatchewan, but from that time forward, the two companies made it a practice to build side by side. In this way, the rivals could watch each other and, in case of Indian attack, there was the possibility of co-operation in staging a defence. But strife was more common than co-operation; sometimes one trader would seize his rival's furs and often there were fights. Colin Robertson, on one occasion, considered it necessary to take 130 armed men to Lake Athabasca to protect his interests, but later he was captured by his opposition and held prisoner.

The North West Company built a post just above the point at which the Sturgeon River enters the Saskatchewan, calling it Fort Augustus. Almost at once, William Tomison of the Hudson's Bay Company built the first Edmonton House, right alongside. After a few years, when the heavy pressure of trapping depleted the local beaver numbers, the two companies moved to build at a riverside location within today's city of Edmonton.

More twin posts were built in 1799, a North West Company fort called Rocky Mountain House and a Hudson's Bay Company establishment called Acton House, both close to the present townsite of Rocky Mountain House.

Being close to the mountains, Rocky Mountain House saw much of early leaders like Duncan McGillivray and David Thompson. It should be noted that the North West Company, anxious to find an outlet offering more economy than the long and costly route to Montreal, encouraged exploration. Alexander Mackenzie, setting out from Fort Chipewyan in 1789, made his way down the river which now bears his name. Following it right to the Arctic, he thought and hoped it would prove to be the long-looked-for route to the Pacific. Four years later, he paddled west on Peace River and other streams and came to the Pacific, the first to cross the continent completely. Still later, Simon Fraser built trading posts in British Columbia country, and in 1808 made his way down the big and dangerous river named after him, eventually reaching the Pacific.

It was with these famous explorers and traders that David Thompson belonged. This man, considered by some observers to have been the greatest map-maker the continent has known, was born in Wales in 1770. At 14 years of age, he came to the Hudson's Bay Company as an apprentice in the trade, in order to learn about the value of furs and dealing with Indians. His ability and high principles were at once evident. He objected to the use of liquor in Indian trade and refused to allow it. He was highly successful in everything he attempted for the Company, but believing that he would have more freedom to explore and make maps if he were with the other company, he resigned and signed on with the North West Company. In the meantine, he married Charlotte Small, daughter of an Irish trader and his Indian wife.

In 1800, and for several successive years, Thompson and his family wintered at Rocky Mountain House, and it was from there that he set out in 1811 on the trip of discovery which took him to the mouth of the Columbia River.

His work in mapping extended far in all directions. One of his notable achievements was the preparation of a master map of the entire West, a priceless document now in the possession of the Royal Ontario Museum in Toronto.

The sad part of the story is that this great man died in poverty and obscurity. After retiring in the East, he used his savings to settle some debts incurred by members of his family and then made a loan for the construction of a church. The church debt was never repaid and, apparently, members of his big family of 13 were not of much help. Prior to his death at the age of 87, he was seen pawning his overcoat to buy food for himself and his wife. For his great service he deserved better.

There were, of course, many other trading centres, most of them built for the express purpose of making profits from beaver skins. When the extent of greedy killing is considered, it is a wonder that these animals survived at all. New areas were dotted by posts such as Chesterfield House built by Peter Fidler on the South Saskatchewan in 1800, Henry House in today's Jasper Park, Fort Vermilion in the north, Fort Dunvegan on Peace River, Piegan Post or Old Bow Ford on the Bow, and others west of the Rockies.

The typical trading post was simple but strong in construction, resistant to attacks from both Indians and business rivals. Since rivers were the only highways, a favourite location for the posts was beside a good stream, perhaps only 50 or 100 yards back from it. Hudson's Bay Company posts were generally square while French posts were oblong. In either case, they had the protection of heavy log palisades, constructed by placing the logs side by side, upright in a trench, to make the walls 10 to 15 feet high. There might be two gates, but the main one opened on the river side. Bastions built along the walls and at the corners gave traders a clear view of the entrance in case of attack and a clear range for shooting if necessary.

Inside the heavy wall of a typical post were several buildings: the chief trader's house, the main structure used in trading, sleeping quarters for assistants and, in some instances, an ice house for storing and freezing buffalo carcasses. There was nothing pretentious about these small, shack-like buildings. Rarely did they have anything better than dirt floors, sod roofs, and stone fireplaces set up without benefit of mortar. Nevertheless, for the wintering partner or chief trader and his helpers the post was home, and they liked it.

The new routes to the Pacific did not prove particularly useful to the traders, but the North West Company did build a number of posts west of the Rockies. The Russians, having discovered millions of fur seals and sea otters in the North Pacific, started the fur trade on that side of the continent. But Captain James Cook, not far behind, was at Nootka Sound on Vancouver Island in 1778, the same year that Peter Pond went to Athabasca. Cook's men obtained some furs from Island Indians, later turning them to handsome profit in China.

Fort McLeod, built by Simon Fraser in 1805, was the first permanent trading post in British Columbia territory but was followed in the next few years by Fort Fraser, Fort St. James, and Fort George, all North West Company ventures.

East of the mountains, competition between the two big and powerful companies became increasingly bitter, and there was often violence. These internal difficulties ended in 1821, however, when the Hudson's Bay Company and North West Company united, retaining the Hudson's Bay Company name. It was over this bigger organization, exercising unchallenged monopoly in trading across the West, that George Simpson, who was later knighted, ruled as governor for many years after the union. He was undoubtedly one of the most colourful as well as most influential figures in the Canadian story.

A familiar picture shows George Simpson's canoe as occupants of trading posts saw it arrive on the occasions of annual tours of inspection. At the paddles were eight tireless *voyageurs*, bending with the clocklike rhythm of 40 strokes per minute while the Governor's private piper, Colin Fraser, stood playing hard on his precious bagpipes at one end of the canoe and George Simpson, wearing plug hat and swallowtail coat, stood in dignity at the other end. No doubt both traders and Indians who saw it were properly impressed.

Although conditions were still primitive, most traders liked the wild, free life in the fur country and hoped it would remain unchanged forever. Except for some simple rules laid down by the Hudson's Bay Company men, no laws existed and this, too, suited the traders well. They wanted no railroad because it would bring settlers, and settlement would be harmful for trapping. They came to accept the small agricultural settlement at Red River but hoped that it would extend no further. Being strongly attached

Sir George Simpson, Governor-in-chief of the Hudson's Bay Company territories during the middle of the nineteenth century. He ruled with a firm hand and established a notable record for administration in almost half a continent.

to the fur trade, they had no trouble convincing themselves that the country would be unsuitable for farming anyway and should be left to the trappers and traders forever.

Some of those men working in the fur trade were responsible for spreading stories about the dangerous severity of climate and the poverty of the soil. George Simpson's men knew that as long as the country could be made to appear worthless for cultivation, they would be left in peace.

Thus it remained until 1869 when, with some fresh views about the West being fit for farming, the Government of Canada bought Rupert's Land from the Hudson's Bay Company and brought to an end the fur trade as it had been carried on for almost 200 years. For the pioneer company, it demanded some major adjustments, but business operations in a somewhat changed form continued without interruption. The 300th anniversary of the Company could not pass without public recognition of its unique position in the life of the West, for no other business organization has been so much a part of Canadian history.

Trading Posts Become Cities

Winnipeg and Edmonton, two of Canada's major cities and both provincial capitals, had their origin in the fur trade. The Manitoba city, a focal point of western history, could claim the longer association with furs because of the la Vérendrye post, Fort Rouge, built in 1738; however, that post was occupied only a short time, and the beginning of permanent settlement on both sites came in the early years of the 19th century.

The North West Company built Fort Gibraltar at the northwest junction of the Red and Assiniboine Rivers about 1804, and the rebuilding of the North West Company's Fort Augustus and the Hudson's Bay Company's Fort Edmonton was in 1813. For the Edmonton area, trade in furs was the only industry for half a century while, in the Manitoba community, the coming of the Selkirk Settlers changed the character of local industry somewhat. In spite of this difference, men living at both places saw about the same sort of activity: Indians arriving to pitch tipis for short periods, singing *voyageurs* coming and going, and millions of beaver pelts being packed in canoes for shipment to markets in far parts of the world. Nobody was thinking about building a city; nobody, until the coming of the settlers, was thinking of anything except the fur trade.

The land beside the Red River had several forts and trading posts. Soon after their arrival in 1812, the Selkirk people built Fort Douglas, at a short distance downstream from Fort Gibraltar. A few years later, Fort Gibraltar was lost by fire, and in 1822, the year after the two companies merged, the Hudson's Bay Company rebuilt it and called it Fort Garry, in honour of Nicholas Garry, Deputy Governor of the Company at the time.

After the rebellious Red River flooded the settlement severely in 1826, Governor George Simpson made plans for a fort on higher ground and, in 1831, he started building Lower Fort Garry on the west side of the river, about 20 miles downstream. It was a big undertaking. The limestone walls alone were seven and one-half feet high and three feet in thickness at the base, representing an enormous building task. Stonemasons were brought from the Hebrides. Here in the Lower Fort, which still stands as a frontier landmark, George Simpson made his home for a few years. While Simpson was there, the Lower Fort was the Hudson's Bay headquarters for the Red River District and, for all practical purposes, the capital of the fur country. It was also a centre of industry inasmuch as it had the only skilled black-smiths in the country.

The presence of the Selkirk Settlers did nothing to hurt Fort Garry as a centre of importance in the fur trade. The growth of farming was very slow, and even as late as 1850, the annual buffalo hunt was contributing more to local food needs than the fields cultivated by settlers.

Fort Garry was a leader in the introduction of newer methods of trans-portation. The local rivers carried Indian canoes fashioned with birch bark, and later the bigger, 25-foot North canoes and York boats which travelled in brigades of from 10 to 30 boats, and which carried most of the Hudson's Bay Company freight. A major change in transportation came with the general acceptance of Red River carts, the first of which were made at Pembina, a short distance south of Fort Garry.

These all-wood vehicles had two wheels and were usually pulled by oxen or horses. At the mid-point of the nineteenth century, about 1,500 of these carts were in use on the trails between Fort Garry and St. Paul, generally travelling in groups or cart trains.

In 1859, after Fort Garry residents rushed to the Red River to see what was causing the strange sound, like somebody blowing in an empty bottle, they saw the first steamboat on that part of the river. It was the riverboat *Anson Northup*. Far removed from a modern steamship, it looked more like a paddlewheel-driven raft carrying an old warehouse. But the *Anson Northup* was the forerunner of an extensive service which was later ex-tended into the Assiniboine and then the Saskatchewan. Ultimately, the riverboats were making calls as far west as Fort Edmonton.

Then, in 1877, just four years after Winnipeg was incorporated as a city, a riverboat brought a most unusual cargo, a railroad locomotive already named *Countess of Dufferin*. The West now had a railroad locomotive, but no railroad. The event did, however, signal the beginning of a big pro-gram of railroad construction and Winnipeg became, more than ever, the Gateway to the West.

At Edmonton the story was somewhat different. The first trading post to carry the Edmonton name was built in 1795, not on the present site of the city of Edmonton, but on the north bank of the Saskatchewan River, about 20 miles downstream from the modern city. Once again it was a case of Hudson's Bay Company and North West Company men building side by side. Early in that year, Angus Shaw of the North West Company selected the site and built about a mile and a half west of where the Sturgeon River emptied into the Saskatchewan. The fort was called Augustus, also Fort des Prairies. It seemed to be the best place Shaw had seen for beavers. Later in the same year, William Tomison of the Hudson's Bay Company followed suit and built the first Edmonton House, honouring the place in Middlesex, England, where Sir James Winter Lake, an officer of the Company, made his home. Cowper, the poet, also made his home there at one time and mentioned the place in verses which immortalized John Gilpin:

> *To-morrow is our wedding-day,*
> *And we will then repair*
> *Unto the Bell at Edmonton*
> *All in a chaise and pair.*

WILLIAM COWPER, John Gilpin

Inside a stout stockade made from pine logs, Tomison supervised the construction of three buildings: a house of 60 feet by 18 feet for his own use, a storage building, and a blacksmith shop. The buildings were well constructed and had the special luxury of stone chimneys.

After a few years, beaver numbers fell drastically because of the greedy trapping. Hoping to find fresh supplies of skins, men of both forts moved westward in the spring of 1802 and built the second Fort Augustus and the second Fort Edmonton on the riverflat. These were the first structures on the site of present-day Edmonton.

The "Countess of Dufferin", the first railroad locomotive brought to the West, now has a place of honour in Winnipeg.

Canadian Pacific Railways

Again and again the traders moved. There was no attempt to practise conservation, and the beaver population in the area fell. By 1810, company representatives were moving to build about 75 miles below the present site of Edmonton. It was only a short distance east of present-day Pakan that the third Fort Augustus and third Fort Edmonton were built.

There was still another move. In 1813, when the fur harvest dropped once more, the two companies moved back to build again on land in today's city of Edmonton. The earlier forts, built low on the riverflats, had been washed away by floods, and the Hudson's Bay Company now built on benchland just below the ground on which the Alberta Legislative Building was constructed. The rival company chose a location closer to the water and near today's Victoria Golf Course.

When the two old companies united in 1821, Fort Edmonton was chosen for continued use while Fort Augustus was soon abandoned. James Bird became the first chief factor after the union, and then John Rowand.

Fort Edmonton was the scene of stirring activities. It was always in a position of danger because of its location in relation to the Indian tribes. Both Blackfoot Indians and Crees came that far north. When braves of the two enemy groups met, battle could be expected, but company men wanted to trade with both tribes, and the risks were accepted.

Trade in furs continued to be the reason for the fort's existence, but boat-building and pemmican-making were sidelines for which the place gained fame. In 1850, there was also a small farm of about 50 or 75 acres under cultivation, on which wheat, barley, and vegetables were grown.

It was Chief Factor Rowand, however, who gave Fort Edmonton its distinctiveness. Rowand was an Irish-Canadian, born near Montreal in 1787, and he started working for the North West Company while still in his teens. He became chief factor at Fort Edmonton in 1823, remaining in the position until his death in 1854. His way with Indians was unusual, for although he tended to bully them, he still won their respect. Rowand had a well-filled medicine chest, which he used freely, thus gaining his reputation as a medicine man. Even the romance leading to his marriage to an Indian girl resembled something from a storybook. One day when he had been hunting, his saddlehorse returned without him. An Indian girl who may have been dreaming about living in his big house suspected trouble and rode out to search for him. She found him but he had a broken leg. After she managed to get him on her horse and bring him back to the fort, she set the fractured limb and cared for him. As a result of her kindness, he married her.

In becoming Mrs. Rowand, the girl soon moved to occupy the biggest house west of Toronto. It was strictly John Rowand's idea and became known as Rowand's Folly. Made from squared logs, it was 70 feet by 60 feet and three stories high. The long balconies were just right for Colin Fraser of the Hudson's Bay Company who liked to pace slowly back and forth as he played his famous bagpipes, filling the river valley with Highland strains.

There were other Rowand innovations, making early Edmonton a place of distinction. The Chief Factor liked racehorses, and when Alexander Ross visited in 1825, Rowand had a two-mile racetrack near the fort. There was also Rowand's famous icehouse, made for storing buffalo meat. It was a big pit in the riverbank and, as soon as the ice was sufficiently thick on the river, men were directed to cut pieces and pile them around the walls. Then, having prepared the ice chamber, Rowand's men went hunting to try to fill the pit with buffalo carcasses. Sometimes buffalo herds were within gunshot of the fort walls; sometimes they were far away. Rowand wanted his meatpit to be full in case of a scarcity in the herds later in the winter, and as many as five or six hundred unskinned carcasses were piled in the icy cave and frozen. The big appetites of 150 or 200 people and many dogs living inside the stockade demanded red meat and lots of it.

Governor George Simpson regarded Rowand as the best of the traders in his farflung fur empire. Everybody knew him as a bustling and vigorous fellow with a fiery temper. It was during a fit of anger while visiting Fort Pitt that he dropped dead. Friends buried him there, but somebody recalled one of Rowand's last requests: namely, that his bones ultimately might rest close to Montreal. George Simpson, who was by this time knighted, authorized that the body be removed and taken to the East, but such an order presented problems at a time when transportation was still at the cart and canoe stage. The story is told that the remains were placed in a barrel containing rum and taken by Sir George Simpson's canoe to Fort Garry. *Voyageurs* were superstitious people, however, and the idea of carrying a dead body or the bones of a dead man produced growing unrest, and to avoid a rebellious refusal to carry the barrel any further, Simpson sent it with a fresh and unsuspecting crew to Hudson Bay, to be taken by sailing ship to London and then rerouted back to Montreal. Finally, after being shipped many thousands of miles by water, John Rowand's bones were laid to rest exactly where the great fur trader had requested.

One of the notable features about both Fort Garry and Fort Edmonton of a century ago was their positions as terminals on the country's main highway which happened to be the water course on Red River, Lake Winnipeg, and Saskatchewan River. There was a cart trail with many deep ruts connecting the two points; however, it was a trail of roughly a thousand miles, and the longer route by water offered cheaper transportation and more comfort for travellers. The latter route seemed to be Nature's provision for the artery needed to support the country's commerce.

Rough water at Grand Rapids, near the mouth of the Saskatchewan, was the most serious obstacle to navigation on the long stretch of water. The river fell 1785 feet over a distance of 1,200 twisting miles, with 275 feet of the drop being in the three miles of rapids close to the river's mouth. It was considered necessary to transfer both riverboat freight and passengers at this point.

They halted to pick up or drop cargo at Cumberland House, Fort la Corne, Prince Albert, Fort Carlton, Battleford, and Fort Pitt. Other planned stops were made to allow members of the crew to go ashore in order to cut cordwood for the boat's ravenous furnaces. There were no icebergs on the route, but there were shallows, rocks, sandbars, and changing streamcourses enough to worry a ship's captain. At best a return trip between Winnipeg and Edmonton would take 30 days. That was a big improvement on Red River cart travel over the distance, which was expected to take four months.

Several shipping companies offered riverboat service between the two old fur-trading centres. The North West Navigation Company, operating mainly on the Winnipeg side of Grand Rapids, had the sternwheeler *Marquette*, the propeller-boat *Colville*, the tugboat *Glendevon*, and the side-wheeler *Princess* which was the luxury boat on the run. The Winnipeg and Western Transportation Company, with the *Northcote, Marquis, Alpha, Lady Ellen*, and *North West*, the latter a double-decker, handled most of the through traffic between Winnipeg and Edmonton. The charge for freight carried all the way varied from $4.00 to $6.50 per hundred pounds, and passengers could travel one way for $40.00 or $20.00, depending on whether or not they demanded some better sleeping accommodation than that offered by the exposed floor of the deck.

Occasionally there were disasters, as in August 1879, when the well-known *Lily*, with the Lieutenant Governor of the Territories among the passengers, struck a rock high on the Saskatchewan and sank. Two muscular Indians carried His Honour and some other distinguished passengers ashore, and no lives were lost.

Riverboats were docking at Fort Edmonton in 1874, the same year as the Mounted Police came to the far West. Inspector W. D. Jarvis and his men arrived at Fort Edmonton on November 1 and wintered there. His intention was to build a police post somewhere in the area, but instead of accepting a site close to Fort Edmonton, he set out early in the spring of 1875 to find a better situation somewhere downstream. The Hudson's Bay Company officials were angry with Jarvis because of his decision to build elsewhere, but he answered their objections by explaining his hope of finding a place offering an easier crossing and one more likely to be suitable for a city. His search took him to the south bank of the river where he constructed Fort Saskatchewan, about opposite where Forts Augustus and Edmonton were built in 1795. Settlers living on the long, narrow river-lot farms thereabout, most of whom had French names, had a vision of a city emerging there. Before long, lots were being laid out and offered for sale in what was to become Saskatchewan City. Under somewhat different circumstances and with a slight shift in fortune, Saskatchewan City might have become the metropolis of central Alberta and the capital of a province, but destiny seemed to favour Fort Edmonton, and Saskatchewan City was soon forgotten.

Frank Oliver came that way, hauling a printing press from Winnipeg, and he printed the first issue of the *Edmonton Bulletin* on December 6, 1880, reporting that "Messrs. Sinclair and McLane have the mail contract from Winnipeg to here, 925 miles, for one year," and that "Sitting Bull is again talking of going south."

Finally, the rails came, signalling the best of all progress. The first trains steamed into Winnipeg in 1878, and Edmonton saw the rails laid to furnish a connection with Calgary in 1891, one year before the old fur capital was incorporated as a town. The incorporation of Edmonton as a city was in 1904 and, in the next year, the Canadian Northern Railway was extended to it.

The most notable strides of progress were yet to come in order to demonstrate how a fur trading community could, in a remarkably short space of time, mature to become a proud and flourishing city with a population approaching 400,000.

3 Pioneers and Adventurers

The Selkirk Settlers

The fur traders were opposed to settlement or agriculture, fearing that it would discourage trapping. On a few occasions, they did cultivate small, garden-size plots of ground for vegetables, but the first genuine attempts at farming were those made by the settlers who came to Lord Selkirk's colony beside the Red River.

The Scottish Earl of Selkirk was a man with strong feelings of sympathy for evicted crofters or any peasant people trying to find security on farms. At an earlier time, he assisted a colony on Prince Edward Island and another called Baldoon in Upper Canada. With faith that the soil of Rupert's Land was better than appraisals by fur traders indicated, Selkirk resolved to start a colony there.

As other Hudson's Bay Company men saw the proposal, it would have only one point of merit: it would be the means of furnishing cheaper flour, cheese, and other provisions for the scattered trading posts, thereby giving the English company an advantage over the North West Company.

Having acquired a big share of stock in the Hudson's Bay Company, Selkirk was able to obtain a land grant of 116,000 square miles for the mere price of ten shillings. He called this Assiniboia, and it included parts of modern Manitoba, Saskatchewan, Ontario, Minnesota, and North Dakota.

Of course, the North West Company frowned on Selkirk's plan for a farming settlement. The Montreal-based company wanted no settlers to interfere with trapping. In addition, the North Westers wanted to think they had a successor's claim to the area opened up by la Vérendrye.

But Lord Selkirk was not one to be dissuaded from doing what he believed to be right, and on July 26, 1811, the first of the Selkirk men, described as the Advance Guard, sailed from Stornoway, Scotland. It was a long and trying voyage by sailing vessel, usually taking 60 days or more, and the danger of scurvy or typhoid fever was ever present. Members of the party wintered at York Factory, where the welcome was said to be nearly as cool as the January weather.

In the spring, the people started over the 730 miles of land and water to where Winnipeg stands today. After a 55-day journey, the 23-member advance guard arrived at the promised land and found it bleak and uninviting. There, the only human inhabitants were the occupants of Fort Gibraltar, the North West Company post.

The newcomers saw their leader, Miles Macdonell, face the North West Company fort, directly across the river, and formally claim the area for the purposes of Lord Selkirk's plan. The only spectators, other than Macdonell's men, were a few Indians who did not know what it was all about and the few servants of the other company who did not like it. After having proclaimed his intentions, Macdonell ordered the firing of his cannon and then the opening of a keg of spirits to mark the occasion.

Macdonell and his men were there to make preparations for the settlers who were to follow shortly. His first problem was to find food and his second to ensure shelter against the oncoming northwestern winter. Since there was very little wild meat to be taken close to the union of the rivers, Macdonell decided to send most of the people to Pembina, keeping back only enough workers to dig a plot of ground for the one and one-half bushels of seed wheat brought from Scotland.

At the upstream location, Macdonell chose a building site on the south side of Pembina River, where it joins the Red, and gave instructions to start building. Indians were hired to hunt buffalo, and a local man described as a Canadian freeman was employed to catch fish, using hooks made from nails.

On October 27, four weeks after Macdonell's arrival, Owen Keveny and his bigger party of 71 persons arrived, compounding the problem of finding food and shelter on an unfriendly frontier. These, like the first to arrive, were directed to Pembina for the first winter and, by the latter part of November, all had moved out of tents into something offering better protection against the cold. Macdonell raised a flag and called the place Fort Daer.

It was a trying winter, but it passed. As soon as spring days were warm enough, settlers returned to the mouth of the Assiniboine to cultivate some ground and build permanent homes on the long and narrow riverlot farms laid out by Peter Fidler. Although lots might extend for two miles back from the river, they were generally only 220 yards wide. This arrangement gave every one a frontage on the river which was the common highway, and it permitted settlers to live closely together to enjoy social advantages and better defence in case of Indian attack.

In spite of their precautions, troubles were far more numerous than anybody could have anticipated. The imported winter wheat failed to mature on this foreign soil, and the peas and barley did no better. Only the potatoes produced a harvest.

More Scottish settlers sailed in 1813, but did not reach the settlement until June 21 of the next year. It was a journey marked by extreme hardship. Although the ocean trip took only 60 days, the two sailing ships were crowded and typhoid fever broke out, causing several deaths. Then, instead of taking the colonists to York Factory where they might have wintered with relative comfort, a contrary ship's captain discharged all passengers at Fort Prince of Wales where there was neither accommodation nor welcome for the newcomers. While some of the immigrants were still feeling the effects of typhoid fever, they were all obliged to tramp upstream beside the Churchill River to build winter quarters for themselves. By shooting partridges, the men managed to provide enough food to see them through.

Anxious to be on their way in the spring, on April 6, 21 of the strongest men and 20 of the strongest women started to walk 150 miles over the snow to York Factory in order to be ready for the longer trip to Red River as soon as the frost was out of the air, and the ice was out of the river. In marching along through the sub-Arctic snow, the proud Scots, weakened as they were, did not fail to have their Highland piper along to keep up lagging spirits. A month after leaving Fort Prince of Wales, those eager pioneers were ready to leave York Factory, still almost 750 miles from their destination.

One pioneer hardship after another presented itself, and those first farmers found many reasons to be discouraged. Some gave up the struggle and left the frontier; others refused to quit. Miles Macdonell conceded that the soil might indeed have some promise for farming. In a report to Lord Selkirk, he said that the country exceeded any idea he had formed of its wealth. He was surprised that it had been left unsettled for so long and felt sure that the availability of both buffalo and fish would help any number of people subsist until their crops matured. The land, he felt, was extremely fertile, and he considered the climate most healthful.

Nevertheless, the small plots of wheat were frozen in 1814 and 1817; grasshoppers destroyed the crops in 1818 and 1819; mice appeared in unprecedented numbers and devoured almost all of the crop in 1825; and floods ruined all chance of crop return in 1826. Even more alarming than crop loss in some of those years was the hostility bordering on warfare between those in charge of the settlement and the North West Company.

The traders from Montreal could think of a score of reasons why the farming settlement should be removed or destroyed. It seemed entirely inconsistent with the business of taking and transporting furs. Indeed, the idea of rivals establishing a farming settlement right across the main trade route to Grand Portage and Montreal and close to the heart of the area furnishing pemmican for company brigades made the North Westers want to fight. To them, the Hudson's Bay Company charter was a worthless thing anyway, and they were not willing to accept interference with their freedom to conduct trade.

At the same time, there were errors in judgement on the side of the Selkirk leaders. After spending two winters at Pembina and having additional colonists to feed, Miles Macdonell issued a proclamation which forbade servants of both trading companies to take pemmican out of Assiniboia. Hudson's Bay Company men surrendered the pemmican they had prepared for shipment westward and, then, Miles Macdonell seized the North West Company's pemmican supplies. Although he was prepared to pay for it, the North Westers took both the proclamation and the seizure as insults and wondered how they might effect complete downfall of the colony, either by fair means or foul.

The North West Company men first tried to induce the settlers to leave. In order to capture Scottish confidence, the great room at Fort Gibraltar rang throughout winter months with the heartwarming music from bagpipes. Some settlers accepted North West Company offers of free transportation by canoe to Upper Canada.

In the spring of 1815, Métis in the employ of the North West Company managed to terrorize the settlers, then burn Fort Douglas, and the 13 remaining families fled to Jack River, at the north end of Lake Winnipeg.

North West Company officers noted the colony's apparent collapse with satisfaction. They were sure it would not be revived; however, another group of settlers under a new governor, Robert Semple, was already travelling toward Red River. Simultaneously, Colin Robertson, with a group of 20 men, came from the East and persuaded members of the 13 frightened families to return from Jack River and rebuild their homes. Consequently, freeze-up in the autumn of 1815 found the colony showing signs of rehabilitation. Some crops were harvested, and sufficient buffalo meat was stored to ensure against winter starvation. Hope had returned to the colony.

But the worst blow of all was struck on June 19, 1816, in the following spring. This tragedy came to be known as the Massacre of Seven Oaks.

Lord Selkirk and Fort Garry in the late 1860's.

The North Westers who admitted hatred for the settlement and the Métis people who resented occupation of lands they considered theirs were ready allies in the war; the traders had no hesitation in using the natives to perform their dirty-work. At the same time, the settlers under the leadership of Robert Semple were not blameless in starting the trouble. After seizing and burning Fort Gibraltar, they might have expected violence. Who actually fired the first shot will always remain in doubt.

The North West Company men were expecting a brigade of canoes to arrive from Grand Portage and feared that it might be prevented from passing the settlement and making its way into the Assiniboine. For that reason, the North Westers explained, they authorized a group of 60 Métis under the capable young Métis, Cuthbert Grant, to ride from the Portage la Prairie area and to serve as an escort for the safe passage of the brigade. After following the Assiniboine until they arrived within sight of the colony, Cuthbert Grant and his men veered in a northeasterly direction with the idea of reaching the Red River at a point below the junction. This was where the trouble started. A boy in the lookout tower of the rebuilt Fort Douglas gave the alarm: "Armed men riding straight for us."

Governor Semple and 30 men of the settlement rode northward on a trail corresponding to Winnipeg's present-day Main Street in order to intercept the intruders and determine their intentions. As he came close to Grant's group, Semple realized he was outnumbered and sent back for reinforcements. But he continued his march until he was face to face with one of Grant's men, Boucher by name. After a few angry words, a shot was fired and the battle began. The natives were good with guns, too good for the settlers, and before long, Governor Semple and 20 of his followers were dead, and the remainder of the Fort Douglas men were prisoners.

It was a shocking hour in the life of the colony, and again the terror-stricken settlers abandoned their Red River homes to seek refuge at the north end of Lake Winnipeg. The North West Company people were happy at the thought that the settlement would never recover from this blow.

But, as fortune would have it, Lord Selkirk was already on his way westward from Montreal with a troop of hired soldiers when he heard the awful news. Even in the previous autumn there had been fear of an armed clash, and Colin Robertson was anxious for help from Selkirk who was then in Montreal. Who would carry the urgent message over such a great distance? Jean-Baptiste Lagimodière, the young fellow with "moose" blood in his legs, the one who had demonstrated skill as a *voyageur*, a hunter, and trader, said he would go. Equipped with snowshoes, gun, and blankets, he left Fort Douglas after snow had blanketed the country in the autumn of 1815 and delivered the plea for help to Lord Selkirk while it was still winter in Montreal.

"Did you walk all the way?" Lord Selkirk asked and Jean-Baptiste replied: "No, I ran most of it." And, to an invitation to remain for a few weeks to rest, the hardy young fellow said he would start back the next morning.

Selkirk acted quickly. Failing to obtain help in the form of armed soldiers from the government of the day, he hired a hundred men from disbanded Swiss and German regiments and began the march which was to end half way across the continent. It was when Selkirk reached Sault Ste. Marie that he heard about the Battle of Seven Oaks.

Directing his anger against the North West Company, he turned the march toward that company's post at Fort William and seized it. Such impulsive action was a mistake, however, and led to a series of court actions in the East where the North West Company had more friends than the earl.

The Selkirk soldiers, called de Meurons, continued on to Red River where, at the beginning of 1817, they recaptured Fort Douglas. With the help of Miles Macdonell who returned at the same time, they induced the settlers to move back from the north. Selkirk spent some time at the colony in the spring of that year and did everything possible to encourage the settlers, even to the point of cancelling debts owing on lands held by them. Sites were fixed for a school and church, and plans were made for roads, bridges, and an experimental farm. The settlers must have known that they had a loyal friend in the earl, one prepared to make every effort to help them.

Before leaving Red River, he signed the first western treaty with local Indians, accepting from Chief Peguis an assurance that his tribesmen were surrendering the land on both sides of Assiniboine and Red Rivers for as far back as a man could see under the belly of a horse on a clear day. This distance was presumably two miles, which was the depth of the narrow riverlot farms surveyed by Peter Fidler.

Back in Montreal, the lawsuits seemed to wear Lord Selkirk down, and he became the victim of tuberculosis. While still making plans for improvements at Red River, he died in France in 1820.

Selkirk's death might have signalled the end for the colony; happily, men of the two big trading companies were now realizing the folly of bitter competition and holding conversations about union. The idea held advantages for both sides and amalgamation was finalized in 1821. No longer would the settlers have reason to fear the North West Company; no longer would the North Westers be denied the right to use the shorter Hudson Bay route to England. And although the Hudson's Bay Company charter gave it monopoly trading rights in Rupert's Land, that is, the region with rivers draining to the bay, an act of parliament in the same year as the union defined the conditions by which an organization could enjoy such exclusive privileges in the regions beyond, meaning those areas with water draining to the north and the Pacific. Almost at once, the reorganized Hudson's Bay Company qualified for the license, giving it control of the western territory extending all the way to the Arctic and Pacific Oceans. It was a control the Company continued to exercise for the next 48 years.

For Red River settlers, still the only farmers in the West, the new security resulting from amalgamation of the companies brought most welcome relief. There was new optimism. Father Provencher and Father Dumoulin came to establish the Roman Catholic Church in 1818, and Rev. John West came as the first Protestant clergyman in 1820. At once, Rev. West built a school which was the first in the West and arranged to hold Anglican church services in it. Three years later, the Catholics did the same, combining both school and church in one building.

Even crops seemed to be better after the grasshopper years, and 1824 was a particularly favourable year for wheat. It was the first year a plow was used, and it was one made in the settlement; however, the new implement did not win immediate popularity because wheat grown on land prepared by spade and hoe far outyielded that which was planted on plowed ground. As reported by Alexander Ross, wheat on hoed ground yielded 68 bushels per acre and only 44 bushels on plowed ground.

But the new land was still capable of providing very bitter disappointments. There was the memorable flood of 1826 which forced settlers to flee. The preceding winter was more severe than usual, depositing a heavy snowfall. The spring thaw came suddenly, and the Red River rose nine feet in one day. Floodwater continued to rise, overflowing banks, inundating homes, and driving settlers to higher ground. The places where people had lived took on the appearance of a big lake. Cattle were driven to higher locations for safety but, one by one, buildings floated away toward Lake Winnipeg, until scarcely a house remained by the time the river reached its highest level on May 21. One observer reported that 47 houses were swept away in an hour. Two men who thought they would be safe for the night on a haystack awakened after a few hours of sleep to find their haystack bed floating like a raft in the middle of the swollen river.

Again settlers asked themselves if they should consider leaving the rebellious Red River forever. A few more did leave, mainly the de Meurons who came with Lord Selkirk's private army. The remainder had to start over again, as many of them had already done several times. It was June before anybody could return to homes by the riverbank and after the middle of June before fields were dry enough for seeding. By then, it was too late for wheat. Altogether, it was a bitter and costly experience but, as stated by Alexander Ross, most settlers were back, resuming work on their cheerless farms, now as bare and naked as on the day they came to the country.

Although it was not the last flood to devastate the Red River Valley, it was the worst one on record, and the Selkirk Settlers did not see another of similar proportions until 26 years later. In the meantime, farming and living continued uneventfully but satisfactorily, and the settlement's permanency ceased to be questioned.

Settlers Need Sheep and Cattle

If the experiment in farming beside the Red River were to be successful, livestock would be needed. The Scottish farming ideals held by most of the settlers required cattle, sheep, horses, and pigs. But how were the requirements to be satisfied in a land where sheep and cattle were practically unknown, and the only domesticated races were horses and dogs of inferior kinds belonging to the Indians? To the Scots in the community, those Indian ponies were poor substitutes for Clydesdales, but they were hardy, fast, and sure-footed, and any horse was better than none.

Actually, the horse family had evolved in America and furnished the foundation stock for other continents. As geologists have noted, the horse's rise on American soil is recorded on the pages of the rocks. From a dwarf form with several toes on each foot, the horse became bigger and faster and was probably among North American animals crossing the Bering Strait when a land bridge existed there. Then, at some time after the race established itself in other parts of the world, it fell upon bad times on its native American soil and died off. The cause of extinction in the Americas is not known, and one can only speculate about the effect that changes in climate, natural enemies, and disease might have produced.

In any case, the American continents became completely horseless and remained so until the Spaniards who followed Columbus brought horses with them. Spanish horses of that time possessed superior quality, and the animals introduced by the adventurers were probably good ones with varied and attractive colours. Some of those horses were abandoned; others escaped and roamed wild, giving rise to the semi-native mustang stock. The Indians, who were quick to see the advantages of horses and to develop their horsemanship, captured mustang stock or stole stock in order to breed for their own needs. Such Indian horse stock was the only kind available for the first farmers in the West, but it served the pioneer needs very well.

It was always Lord Selkirk's intention that the settlement at Red River become self-supporting as soon as possible. He knew that livestock would be required, and he considered the domestication of the buffalo to be entirely practical. With this in mind, he issued orders to have the plan tested. Evidently, settlers did capture and rear some buffalo calves, but there is nothing to show that the effort was successful.

An exact record of the first cattle brought to the prairie country does not exist, but it is known that a few animals might have been found at scattered trading posts before the coming of settlers. They were probably brought from the Old Country as calves, when they could be transported by canoe with the least difficulty.

It was no easy matter to move cattle or any livestock to a remote place like Red River. Miles Macdonell was known to have sailed away from Stornoway in July 1811, leaving on the dock behind him the eight young cattle intended for the Selkirk Settlement, convinced that it would be inadvisable to carry the necessary water and feed.

Of the few cattle in the West, however, two representatives of the species were at Oxford House, and Macdonell and his men, travelling from Hudson Bay to Red River, took possession of them, adding the young bull and yearling heifer to the canoe freight for the new settlement. Travelling partly by canoe and partly overland, the two young cattle, called Adam and Eve, completed the journey without mishap.

In the following spring, Peter Fidler negotiated for the purchase of additional cattle owned by the North West Company at its post on the Assiniboine. A cow, heifer, and bull were bought for a total price of £100. Including a calf from Adam and Eve, there were now six head of cattle in the settlement, but there was misfortune ahead. The bull bought from the North West Company became vicious and had to be slaughtered; in February 1814, the other bull, Adam, disappeared and was not seen again until his dead body was identified on a piece of ice when the river breakup occurred in the spring.

For several years, just about every effort to increase the size of the Red River herd failed, and the settlers were becoming impatient. In 1816, however, Lord Selkirk resolved to send someone as far south as necessary to find and buy cattle. He wanted to hire a man who would go all the way to Texas if necessary. It was not until June 1819 that a contract was signed with Michael Dousman, an American trader with thorough knowledge of the Mississippi country, to drive in 76 cows at $80 each, 20 oxen and 4 bulls at $100 each, and 6 mares and a stallion.

The Dousman herd was to be delivered at Big Stone Lake at the head of St. Peter's River, but there were numerous obstacles, including passports and an American law which forbade grazing in Indian territory. The cattle, numbering 200, were started from St. Louis in the next spring, but Dousman's men failed to connect with the Selkirk men and, after wintering in the northern region of the United States, all but 19 cattle were dead.

Dousman returned for another herd, but it fell victim to hungry Sioux Indians. By this time, Red River pessimism about ever having cattle was great indeed. The human population had risen, but the total number of livestock at Red River in the spring of 1822 was small for an ambitious farming community: only 45 cows, 3 bulls, 6 oxen, 39 calves, 12 pigs, and 11 sheep.

Nevertheless, Dousman was not one to give up readily. He went again to the far south, and on August 28, 1822, the first successful drive of southern cattle arrived in Fort Garry, at the end of a thousand-mile trail. The delivery of 170 head marked the beginning of a system of farming which appealed to the settlers who had learned the principles of agriculture in the Old Country.

Selkirk's settlers wanted sheep about as much as they wanted cattle, for sheep would provide both meat for food and wool for homespun clothing. Lord Selkirk was well aware of the Scottish crofter's interest in sheep and sent 21 Spanish Merinos with the settlers in 1812. The Merino was a superior wool breed, and there seemed a chance that the settlement might find it practical and profitable to export wool to Britain. The imported Merinos brought nothing but disappointment, however. Beween dogs, coyotes, and lack of care from the settlers, no sheep survived beyond the first year.

For almost 20 years no further attempt was made to establish sheep in the colony, but the farmers continued to talk hopefully about getting flocks and producing their own wool. Finally, in 1832, something was done about it. The Hudson's Bay Company made funds available, and late in the year a party headed by W. G. Rae, a Company clerk, prepared to travel as far south as necessary in order to find and buy sheep. Robert

Campbell, a member of the party, kept a diary and left a complete account of the expedition.

The sheep-buying expedition, with two carts and several saddle-horses, left Fort Garry on November 8, travelling along the east side of the Red River, where there would be less risk of encountering hostile Indians. Beyond Pembina, however, the travellers entered country where the Indians were believed to be the boldest, but they pressed on, starting each day at 3 a.m. and eating breakfast after a few hours on the trail. The halt for their evening meal was at sundown and, after cooking supper, they would move a few miles further before making camp for the night, in order to safeguard against the danger of Sioux Indians being attracted by smoke from a mealtime campfire. According to Robert Campbell, the Red River men knew they were being followed by Indians for several days, but they managed to elude the pursuers and escape a scalping party.

It had been the leader's hope to connect with one of the Mississippi riverboats before freeze-up, thus shortening the travelling time to St. Louis. The travellers missed the last boat of the season, however, and had to continue with horses. By this time, the country was in the grip of winter, and the men awakened some mornings to find themselves buried in snowdrifts.

Fifty-six days later, they reached St. Louis, after a trail of about 1,500 miles from home, but no sheep could be bought at this place. The only advice the local people could offer was to continue on to Kentucky; therefore, the men from the North took to the trail again and finally reached Kentucky where they were able to buy about 1,300 sheep and lambs. On May 3, 1833, the shepherds turned the big flock toward Fort Garry and started on what must have been one of the most notable sheep drives in world history.

As might have been expected, there were many obstacles. Mosquitoes were numerous and hungry; heat became intense; rattlesnakes were said

Ashdown Johnson

Sheep on a western ranch today. The first attempts to raise sheep in the West were unsuccessful, and sheep farming has never attained the popularity of cattle raising.

to have killed a few sheep; and by June, the men were encountering the worst menace of all: speargrass. After crossing the Mississippi, they halted and clipped all the sheep and lambs, hoping to reduce the chance of grass spears penetrating skins and flesh. Already, however, many of the sheep were suffering from festering wounds, aggravated by maggots.

Losses continued to be heavy as the dwindling flock was driven northward at about 12 miles per day. Strangely enough, none of the losses could be attributed to the Sioux Indians who watched the sheep pass and were filled with curiosity at these strange animals. The Indian willingness to let the flock go through unharmed may have been due to a sense of surprise or to the chief's favour which the men bought with the gift of one horse.

On September 16, after 136 days of hard driving, the men arrived at Fort Garry, with what remained of an original flock of 1,300 sheep. Although only 251 of the animals reached the settlement, it is a wonder that any survived. Now, at least, the settlement had a foundation flock from which to raise sheep in numbers suitable for local needs. Here is further evidence that the frontier had men who were ready to accept any challenge, no matter how difficult.

The Summer Buffalo Hunt

Much as the Selkirk Settlers wanted to raise wheat, cattle, and other food-yielding crops, they knew their greatest security was in the buffalo herds, nearly always present in great numbers somewhere to the west. Without buffalo meat and pemmican in the early years, settlers along the Red River would have starved, and even after they were growing grain and raising cattle, the summer hunt continued to be the most important single enterprise of the year, for it was more rewarding than growing wheat and more entertaining than a canoe race. It was as much a community effort as a round-up in the years of open range and one which no able-bodied adult, either male or female, would care to miss.

In its purpose, it was similar to an agricultural harvest, and settlers hoped for good yields. A successful hunt meant food reserves for the months to come, because any meat which was not to be consumed almost at once, while still fresh, was dried and converted into pemmican.

Organized along the lines of any armed manoeuvre, the summer hunt came under strict and clever leaders, who were usually Métis. Immigrant settlers and the native Métis, although living at separate locations on the river, went on the annual hunt together. For about a month each year, scarcely anyone remained in the settlement.

Prejudices arose in later years, but in the first years of the hunt the ablest halfbreed hunters had almost unanimous support for the roles of leadership. The most celebrated of the chief captains was Cuthbert Grant, after he was largely forgiven for his part in the Massacre of Seven Oaks.

The annual hunt began in a small way soon after the Selkirk people arrived, and it became bigger and more imposing as the years passed. In 1820, 540 Red River carts went out for the hunt. By 1830, there were 820 carts, and in 1840, the total reached 1210.

At the midpoint of the century, the Red River buffalo hunt was still the biggest annual event in the lives of settlers. Father Lacombe was one of those who went along in the year 1850, and he told of seeing over a thousand men, women, and children, hundreds of ponies and oxen, an undetermined number of hungry mongrel dogs, and between 800 and 1,000 carts. The hunting fortunes in that particular year were not good; the herds happened to be far away and hunters took only 600 buffaloes. From 1820 to 1840, the years of heaviest slaughter, according to Henry Hind's estimate, settlers killed a total of 652,000 buffaloes. The figure must have included more than the animals taken in the annual summer hunt but, in any case, it is a staggering total.

For the best description of the Red River hunt, the reader should look to the record left by Alexander Ross. The hunt of 1840, Ross tells, began on June 15, with 1,650 men, women, and children in the camp when the roll-call was taken at Pembina three days after leaving Fort Garry. On this occasion, somebody took time to count the dogs, of which there were 542. No doubt these half-starved brutes looked forward to a time of good eating about as much as the men and women.

When camp was made at night, tents were arranged inside an orderly circle made with the carts. The ring of carts furnished a place in which to hold horses and oxen, as well as a barricade in case of attack by Indians.

One of the first orders of business when the cavalcade was ready to move was to elect a leader. Ten captains were chosen and then the chief captain with all the authority of a field marshal in a military campaign. In 1840, the year of which Alexander Ross wrote, the chief captain was again a Métis, Jean-Baptiste Wilkie.

Of course, there had to be rules to govern the participants' conduct both in camp and while hunting. These were generally set down in order to remove all doubt about the consequences for any man who broke the Sabbath or refused to co-operate in maintaining order.

Rules governing the hunt varied little from year to year. Early in the morning, the camp flag was raised to notify all concerned that the cavalcade would start in half an hour. At intervals during the day, the flag was lowered briefly to allow the horses and oxen to rest and, at six o'clock in the evening, the flag was brought down as a signal to make camp for the night.

The rules set down in 1840 were as follows:

1. No buffalo to be run on the Sabbath day.
2. No party to fork off, lag behind, or go before without permission.
3. No person or party to run buffalo before the general order.
4. Every captain with his men in turn to patrol the camp and keep order.
5. For the first trespass against these rules, the offender to have his saddle and bridle cut up.
6. For the second offence, the coat to be taken off the offender's back and cut up.
7. For the third offence, the offender to be flogged.
8. Any person convicted of theft, even to the value of a sinue, to be brought to the middle of the camp, and the crier to call out his or her name three times, adding the word 'thief' at each time.

On this particular expedition, the first big herd was sighted on the twentieth day out, some 250 miles from Fort Garry. The order was given to make camp and prepare for the attack upon the animals.

On the morning of the big day, 400 mounted men waited for the signal to advance. Ross wrote:

At 8 o'clock, the whole cavalcade broke ground and made for the buffalo, first at a slow trot, then at a gallop and lastly at full speed. . . . When the horsemen started, the cattle might have been a mile and a half ahead but they had approached to within four or five hundred yards before the bulls curved their tails and pawed the ground. In a moment more, the whole herd took flight and horses and riders are presently seen bursting in among them; shots are heard and all is smoke, dust and hurry.

ALEXANDER ROSS, *The Red River Settlement*, Smith, Elder & Co., 1856

It was a wild scene. Rough ground, stray bullets, and intense excitement combined to create dangers for men and horses as well as for the buffalo. No doubt the pounding of heavy feet on dry sod sounded like thunder. The constant discharge of guns was deafening as the hunters reloaded their noisy flintlocks without breaking the dangerous speed. The mere fact of reloading guns while the hunters rode at a fast gallop was dangerous enough in itself. Extra lead balls for the guns were carried in the rider's mouth and, in the excitement of the moment, it was quite possible to swallow one or more. Now and then a man came into the path of a stray bullet, although more often than not it was the horse which became injured. A few horses were struck by bullets; some broke legs when they stepped into holes; others were gored by wounded buffalo bulls.

A good hunter on a good horse might get ten or twelve animals in one drive, while another did well to get two or three. It would seem that on this particular day the men from Red River averaged three buffalo each.

Ross continued:

> On this occasion, the surface was rough and full of badger holes. Twenty-three horses and riders were at one moment all sprawling on the ground; one horse gored by a bull was killed on the spot; two more were disabled by the fall. One rider broke his shoulder-blade and another burst his gun and lost three fingers by the accident; and a third was struck on the knee by an exhausted ball. These accidents will not be thought over numerous considering the result, for in the evening no less than 1,375 tongues were brought into camp.
>
> ROSS, *Red River Settlement*, 1856

When the shooting ended and the dust subsided, the hunters sometimes condescended to help skin the slaughtered animals; just as often, they retired to the camp to boast of their successes and celebrate, leaving the women and children to proceed with the unromantic work of skinning and dressing the carcasses and preparing the meat for drying.

The curing of hides and drying of meat for pemmican had to be done in the field, and this required days. Then, if fat from the recently slaughtered animals was rendered and at hand and saskatoon berries were available in the area, it was possible to make pemmican and pack it in buffalo stomach bags before the great annual adventure ended, and the cavalcade of loaded carts, tired horses, and bloated dogs turned toward Fort Garry and home.

The Prairie Explorers: Hind and Palliser

Fur traders gave the impression that the West had no use except for producing beaver skins and buffalo robes, but in the East and in far-away London, there was suspicion that this was wishful thinking on the part of men who made their living from furs. Maybe their love for the 200-year-old industry had blinded them to alternative uses for the country.

The questions requiring attention were very simple ones. Would settlement beyond the Red River be possible and practical, in spite of the opinions held by George Simpson? Could agriculture be expected to succeed in any part of it or must the vast Northwest remain a fur preserve forever? Factual information was needed and the years from 1857 to 1859 were full of probing for fresh answers to old questions.

The government of the province of Canada, that is, Upper and Lower Canada, had no authority in Rupert's Land, but it had an understandable interest and saw fit to appoint Henry Youle Hind, Professor of Chemistry and Geology at The University of Trinity College, to conduct a study. Hind started out boldly in 1857 but did not get beyond the bounds of present-day Manitoba in the first year. In the second year he planned to go to more distant parts. Residents around Fort Garry watched with amused interest as Hind loaded five Red River carts and a wagon with supplies considered necessary: 1,000 pounds of flour, 400 pounds of pemmican, 1,000 rations of "Crimea vegetables", one sheep, three hams, pickles, chocolate, wine, and brandy. To reinforce food reserves still further, Hind was taking along an ox which would pull a cart until such time as a meat scarcity occurred.

The expedition left Fort Garry on June 14. Before long, its members were following the Qu'Appelle Valley westward to its source, close to the Elbow of the South Saskatchewan. There, Hind sensed the possibility of building a dam 85 feet high and 800 yards long, to divert the South Saskatchewan into the Qu'Appelle Valley. It would have meant sending the water over the same course probably taken by the great volumes of water leaving a southern front of Ice Age glaciers.

Hind had no thought of irrigation or hydro power generation; his mind was set most enthusiastically on the idea of providing steamboat communication on a long river route between Fort Garry and the foothills. Perhaps, in his dreams, he saw a water highway linking Winnipeg and Calgary, providing transportation for freight and passengers and making a costly railroad less of a necessity.

In any case, Henry Youle Hind had a vision of a dam close to the site of the huge South Saskatchewan River Dam which was finally completed in 1967. This dam is 210 feet high, and it has created an artificial lake with a 475-mile shoreline. And, although carried away by his enthusiasm for a water highway, he made some useful observations about the area. He could see a good agricultural future for the Park Belt and was moderately optimistic about the prairies, more optimistic certainly than John Palliser who was conducting his appraisal at the same time.

Captain John Palliser, servant of the British government, gave a clear impression of pessimism about the prairie country, but in winning public interest, his observations and reports were much more successful than those of Hind. Every time there is a very dry year on the plains, students refresh themselves on Palliser and express admiration for the accuracy with which he defined the area most likely to suffer from recurring droughts.

Members of the government in London, England, realized they needed guidance. They knew the views of the Hudson's Bay Company officials who would be happy to continue to treat the Northwest, right to the Pacific Ocean, as their private property for another hundred or two hundred years. But the time had come for an independent appraisal. They needed information, reliable information, about climate, soil, and other resources, and about the suitability of the land for settlement.

The Selkirk Colony was 45 years old when the British government commissioned Palliser to examine that portion of the Northwest lying south of the North Saskatchewan River and between the Red River and the Rocky Mountains. The choice of a leader for the expedition was a good one. Palliser was well educated, and because he had hunted buffalo on the American plains, he was not a total stranger in the area. He was an Irishman by birth, an engineer by training, and a bachelor by circumstances; he was also the best man for the job at hand.

The instructions delivered to Palliser were quite specific. He was to observe the physical features of the country, forest resources, coal and other minerals, quality of the soil, and general suitability of the country for farming. He was also to exercise all possible economy in spending government money and all reasonable caution in avoiding Indian scalping knives. As if it were an afterthought on some civil servant's part, he was to "endeavour to ascertain whether one or more practical passes exist over the Rocky Mountains within British territory", suitable for either a wagon road or railroad.

After a lengthy journey from the East by way of Lake Superior, the Palliser party arrived at Lower Fort Garry on July 11, 1857. This group was comprised of well-qualified scientists such as a geologist, geographer, engineer, botanist, and astronomer. In addition, the leader hired some Métis helpers at £40 per year. He was glad to have on his staff some men who knew the country, understood the Indians, and were good with guns. To transport equipment and supplies, he bought some horses at £20 each, five Red River carts, and two small wagons.

Leaving Fort Garry on July 20, Palliser and his men zigzagged their way southwestward and then northwestward to end the first season at Fort Carlton. They continued to criss-cross both prairie and park country, digging holes to test the soil and making written observations about everything in the landscape, and they terminated the second season at Fort Edmonton. Late in 1859, Palliser was making his way westward to the Pacific Coast whence he would sail for England.

The Palliser Report, which appeared a few years after the leader's return to London, was the work of an observer who missed nothing. For students of western history, it will be a source of interest forever. But what did it hold for those people who were awaiting a judgement about the country?

Most obviously, he had nothing very cheerful to say about the prairies. He probably saw the prairies when they were feeling one of the recurring periods of severe drought. "Wherever we struck out on the broad prairie," he wrote, "we generally found the soil worthless, except here and there...." It may have been an error on the part of Palliser to judge the soil by the vegetation growing on it. Where he observed shortage of wood, absence of surface water, and shortness of grass, he made unfavourable conclusions about the area's suitability for cropping.

It is easy to be critical of the way he assessed some of the evidence, but he was strikingly successful in mapping the area likely to suffer most severely from drought. As Palliser saw it, the area which is now known as the Palliser Triangle forms an extension of the Great American Desert. The base of the famous triangle was along the 49th parallel and extended from longitude 100° to 114° West. The apex of the triangle would be at the 52nd parallel of latitude. Significantly, the lines of the triangle enclosed an area which has indeed experienced severe drought rather often, but the area has also been the source of many world wheat championships.

Although no booster for the prairies, Palliser became quite enthusiastic about the Park Belt, which he called the "fertile belt". He was even more glowing in his appreciation of the Cypress Hills, an "oasis on the prairies". There, where rainfall was heavier, he noted different vegetation, animals, and birds.

Perhaps the small farm operated in conjunction with Fort Edmonton helped to convince Palliser of the suitability of Park Belt soils for farming. In any event, he recommended that these Park Belt areas be settled first.

> Almost everywhere along the course of the North Saskatchewan are to be found eligible situations for agricultural settlement; a sufficiency of good soil is everywhere to be found; nor are these advantages merely confined to the neighbourhood of the river. . . . In almost every direction around Edmonton, the land is fine, except only the hilly country at the higher level, such as Beaver Hills.

As for cattle, Palliser recognized some opportunities in the short prairie grass. He may have realized that where the quantity of grass was low, the quality was high. Pigs and sheep might be successful, he reasoned, but he was worried about the devastation which might result from natural enemies such as wolves.

The best summary of his observations comes from his own pen:

> The territory which has now been examined and mapped by this expedition ranges from Lake Superior to the eastern shore of the lesser Okanagan Lake, and from the boundary line to the water shed of the Arctic Ocean. This large belt of country embraces districts, some of which are valuable for the purposes of the agriculturists, while others will forever be comparatively useless.

Palliser's report did not settle all the arguments about the future of the fur country, but it was a useful contribution. Even such restrained optimism for agriculture came, at that time, as something of a shock to many people who had convinced themselves that the West was barren land with no other future than that to which the fur traders had been relegating it.

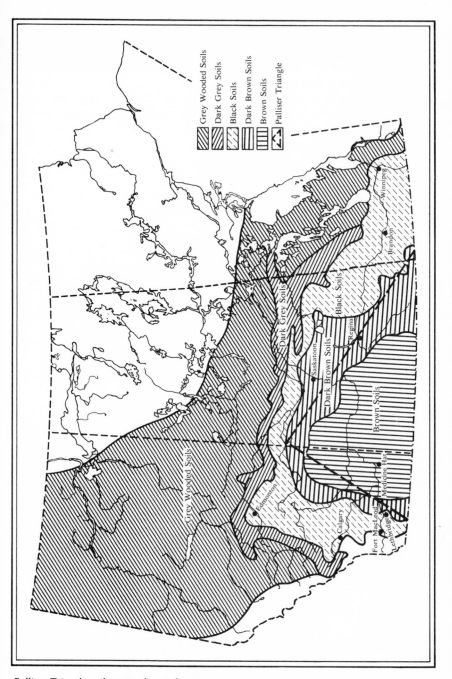

Palliser Triangle and surrounding soil areas.

As those who take time to study the famous Palliser Report will realize, the man's observations went far beyond soil and settlement. He suggested reservations for Indians; he proposed a mounted police force for law enforcement; he favoured rigid liquor laws. Also, Palliser and his men found passes in the mountains which would be suitable for wagon roads or railroads.

It was the first broad technical survey for the West and deserved to be treated as a landmark.

West of the Rockies

Europeans were slow in finding the British Columbia country. Loyal citizens of Canada's most westerly province will find it difficult to understand how so much natural beauty and such wealth in resources could have escaped attention for so long. One obstacle was the distance by sea; another, the mountain barriers on the land route. In any case, exploration and occupation on the west coast came much later than it did on the east side, and the conflicts there, instead of being between England and France, were between England, Russia, and Spain.

In 1778, when Captain James Cook, who was making his third trip around the world, landed at Nootka, on the west coast of Vancouver Island, he was the first white man to set foot on what is now the province of British Columbia. But this was 243 years after Jacques Cartier sailed up the St. Lawrence and visited Stadacona and Hochelaga, the Indian villages which gave rise to Quebec City and Montreal. It was 24 years after Anthony Henday saw the Rockies from the prairie side.

Eight years after Cook's call, a trader, James Strange, had enough imagination to claim the country formally for Britain. To strengthen the claim, he left his ship's doctor, John MacKay, on Vancouver Island to live with the Indians and become the first white man to cultivate British Columbia soil.

Spanish traders were attracted to the island's west coast and wanted it. Conflict of interest brought Spain and England to the brink of war. Finally, however, Spain withdrew and the Nootka Sound Convention of 1791 took Captain George Vancouver to the area. When he was not searching for a water route between the Pacific and Atlantic Oceans, he was charting the west coast. He was there for three years and was the first to circumnavigate the island which now bears his name. Simultaneously, Alexander Mackenzie was crossing the mountains and coming upon the Pacific at Bella Coola.

The Russians were the first to sense that there was a fortune to be made in furs along the continent's west coast. Sea otters in the North Pacific waters were the chief source of Russian interest, and British and American adventurers were attracted before very long. Because no water from the British Columbia watersheds drained to the Great Bay of the North, however, the Hudson's Bay Company had no special privileges until some years later, and it remained for the North West Company to pioneer the intermountain fur trade.

Simon Fraser built Fort McLeod in 1805 and, three years later, he went from Fort George to make the historic trip to the mouth of the big and, in places, treacherous river now carrying his name. About the same time, David Thompson, also for the North West Company, was exploring the Columbia, all the way to where it emptied into the Pacific.

Arriving at the mouth of the Columbia in 1811, Thompson found that John Jacob Astor, founder of the Pacific Fur Company, had been there ahead of him and had built Fort Astoria in the previous year. It looked like a strategic place for a trading post and Thompson was impressed. Two years later, while the War of 1812 was in progress, the North West Company bought Fort Astoria. This post, deep in today's state of Washington, gave the Canadian company a practical, although not complete, control of the west coast trade in furs from Astoria to Alaska. While the North West Company was purchasing Fort Astoria, both the Pacific Fur Company and the North West Company were building trading establishments at the present site of Kamloops. The first permanent post on the coast of today's British Columbia mainland was Fort Langley, built by the Hudson's Bay Company in 1824.

Since the boundary between British North America and territory claimed by the expanding United States was as yet very uncertain, nobody was sure which country would have the best claim to the Lower Columbia River. The boundary dispute proved to be long and bitter. After the two old fur trading companies united in 1821, the reorganized Hudson's Bay Company inherited the brunt of the quarrel but was backed by the might of Britain in its insistence that the Columbia River should be the boundary.

The Americans, on the other hand, contended that the boundary should be far to the north in what is now the province of British Columbia, and James Polk was elected to the presidency of the United States on the familiar slogan of "fifty-four forty or fight". The Americans appeared serious about fighting for what would have given them a big part of today's British Columbia, but a compromise settlement in 1846 fixed the boundary at an extension of the 49th parallel to the coast, and Vancouver Island was to remain a British possession.

The Hudson's Bay Company appeared to anticipate the loss of the Lower Columbia River country and, in 1843, built Fort Victoria at the south end of Vancouver Island, apparently with some plan to make it the west coast headquarters if necessary. It was increasingly evident that if British interests were to resist growing pressures from United States expansion on the west coast, there would have to be some strengthening of positions. Accordingly, the Crown Colony of Vancouver Island was declared in 1850, and Richard Blanshard was named as the first governor.

Blanshard must have had a rough time because the island's white residents were almost exclusively servants of the Hudson's Bay Company, all of whom looked upon Chief Factor James Douglas, a domineering man in any circle, as the highest local authority. After two years, Blanshard resigned and Douglas succeeded as governor. The change placed the island colony, for all practical purposes, under the rule of the Company.

Like the more recent oil find at Leduc, the discovery of gold on the Fraser and Thompson Rivers changed the fortunes of the country. When the news about gold reached San Francisco, the mad scramble started. Miners and would-be miners by the thousands made their way to Victoria and then the mainland. It was quite beyond the constitutional authority of Governor Douglas to cope with the rising problems. A new jurisdiction was needed urgently, quickly, and the British Colonial Office acted to create a new colony, the Crown Colony of British Columbia, with James Douglas as its governor.

The formal declaration setting up the colony was issued at Fort Langley, on November 19, 1858. There the new governor was sworn in, making him the most powerful figure in the country. Sworn in as Chief Justice was Mathew Baillie Begbie, who carried out his duties with rare distinction.

This occurred at the same time as Captain John Palliser's second season of exploration on the prairie side of the mountains. Primitive conditions existed on both sides, but the new urgency for law and order was greater on the British Columbia side. Judge Begbie, who became known as the Hanging Judge, devoted himself to this challenge with success that drew praise from far parts of the world. He was uncompromising in dispensing justice, and it was not long before potential criminals were changing their ideas about lives of sin. No wrongdoer wanted to appear before Judge Begbie, and for a country overrun with miners and men who came to mine the miners, the amount of crime was remarkably small.

Scarcely less challenging was the task of providing roads and works for the suddenly developing need. This, in large measure, became the responsibility of Col. R. C. Moody and his Royal Engineers. Beginning in 1862, the Engineers were making a new road inland from Yale, a formidable task for men with nothing more modern in the way of aids than horses, scrapers, picks, and shovels. It was also a giant economic commitment for a colony with a population of only 25,000, most of them gold rush transients.

The road had to be taken from Yale, the head of navigation on the river and the point at which the Hudson's Bay Company built a fort in 1848, to the junction of the Thompson, along the Thompson to Cook's Ferry, later Spence's Bridge, thence to Ashcroft, northward to Clinton, and then to follow the older Harrison Trail to Soda Creek and on to Barkerville. To anyone lacking James Douglas' resolution, the rockbound country interspersed with mountain ranges and deep gorges would have appeared frightening and hopeless. Nevertheless, the Cariboo Road was completed.

Until the time of the gold rush, British Columbia was still wilderness, with only the slightest evidence of anything as advanced as agriculture. The Spaniards may have cultivated a small amount of ground at Nootka, and some barley, potatoes, and turnips were grown at Fraser Lake in 1811. After the amalgamation of the two old fur companies in 1821, Governor George Simpson ordered that farms be started at trading posts as a means of reducing expenditures for imported food supplies.

The total agricultural effort was still small. Expansion was stalled by the lack of markets, and the first real encouragement came at the midpoint of the century when farmers around Fort Victoria found they could sell wheat, butter, and meat for shipment to Alaska. The best incentive came when 25,000 men with big appetites flocked into the country in the hope of finding gold. Farmers were immediately able to sell all the food and fodder they could produce. Some Vancouver Island farmers moved to the mainland in order to locate close to their market. It was enough to put the situation in the Interior to the test. In 1858, at the very onset of the gold rush, Father Pandosy started a mission 400 miles inland, on the east side of Okanagan Lake, and saw some of the people who accompanied him settling to farm around his Okanagan Mission. They were the first farmers in the Okanagan Valley.

The gold rush makes a proper chapter in itself, but while miners were coming and going, the two coastal colonies were experiencing change. The influx of miners from the south increased the threat of American annexation and the need for consolidation. Yet it was not until the gold rush was declining and most of the miners were drifting away that the island and mainland colonies were united, on November 19, 1866, to form the new colony of British Columbia. Strange as it may seem, the territorial boundaries of the colony were then exactly the same as those of the present province of British Columbia.

New Westminster, at first called Queensborough, was Col. R. C. Moody's choice as the capital of the united colony, but soon thereafter, in 1868, the location of the capital was changed to Victoria, where it remained after British Columbia became a province.

Gold in the Interior

British Columbia gold became a topic of conversation for the first time in 1850, when a discovery was reported in the Queen Charlotte Islands. More important and fantastic, however, were stories from the Interior, telling of Indians who had taken nuggets to Hudson's Bay Company posts, offering to trade them for beads.

The discovery strike was made at Hill's Bar on the Fraser, between Fort Yale and Fort Hope, in March 1858. This was the placer works which filled men with dreams of riches and started the famous rush. During the last half of the year, the Hill's Bar sand yielded over a half a million dollars in gold.

News travelled slowly at a time of primitive communication, but stories of gold on the Fraser and its tributaries ultimately reached distant parts, and people of many races prepared to seek their fortunes. Thousands came from San Francisco and other points in the United States; some came from England, Scotland, and Ireland, sailing round the southern tip of South America and up the west coast; others came from Upper and Lower Canada and Nova Scotia by various routes. At least 25,000 of them came to a part of the world which was far from being ready to receive them. There had been nothing quite like the gold rush to the Cariboo.

The incoming miners went from one river bar to another, prospecting and panning. A few were striking it rich, while the majority were recovering less than enough to pay their expenses. One of the strikes widely discussed at the time was at William's Creek, where William Dietz was the discoverer. In two years, almost four million dollars' worth of gold was taken from William's Creek area alone. Still, the search spread and important finds were reported from Vancouver Island, Okanagan Valley, and points well to the north.

News of fresh discoveries reached the outside and the rush revived. The new interest was in William's Creek, and wave upon wave of fortune-seekers came in. Men in the Canadian East and the eastern United States sensed a possible advantage in a direct route across the continent. They could travel by rail to St. Paul in Minnesota, by stage coach to a point on the Red River, and then by steamboat to Fort Garry. That was the course chosen by the group known as the Overlanders, but it was not as easy as the map made it appear.

The completely new riverboat, *International*, which was 150 feet long and which drew 42 inches of water, arrived on her maiden voyage in May 1862, with a cargo of freight and a crowd of eager miners on their way to the gold fields of the Cariboo. There, at Fort Garry, about 130 of them, dreaming about scooping up fortunes in gold, prepared for the long and trying trip across a thousand miles of prairies and some hundreds of miles of mountain country.

It was June when they started overland. With an Ontario man, Tom MacMickling, as leader, the party left the Red River settlement in horse-drawn and ox-drawn carts. In the party was one woman, Mrs. August Schubert, with three children. It was a poor place for a woman, but there she was, showing no less courage and determination than the men. They knew there were dangers ahead. The temper of prairie Indians left much to be desired and there was no guarantee of food supplies, but the men were armed and ready to use their guns.

Each night the travellers camped within a circle made by carts. Guards were posted to maintain constant watch for attackers. Each morning at two o'clock, the camp was roused for the day's journey. Periodically, the men hunted buffalo and made pemmican, prairie-style.

The Overlanders reached Fort Edmonton about a month after leaving Fort Garry and faced a delay of several weeks while preparations were made for what was recognized as the most difficult part of the expedition: their advance into and beyond the Yellowhead Pass. Carts and wagons were abandoned in favour of pack horses and pack oxen, 140 animals altogether, each loaded with about 200 pounds of equipment and supplies. By the time they reached the pass, pemmican and other food reserves were depleted, and the travellers were obliged to fall back on meat provided by the slaughter of work oxen.

At this point, they faced an important decision about their route. Indians told them they might follow the Fraser River as it swung northward before bearing south again. Other advice was to go overland and cross some mountains with the idea of coming to another river, the North Thompson. Members of the party could not agree, and they divided their resources, separating into two groups. One group set about building rafts 40 feet in length, with which to float down the Fraser, while the others in the party took the 130 remaining horses and oxen and set out through the forests and over mountain obstacles, heading mainly southward.

Those following the Fraser reached Quesnel on September 11. The others encountered more obstacles, but after rafting down the North Thompson, they arrived at Fort Kamloops on October 13, thankful to be nearing the end of their journey. On the morning after arriving at Kamloops, Mrs. Schubert's new baby was born, the first white child born at that old trading centre.

Althogether, it was a rough trip, and lives were lost on the fast waters of both the Fraser and the Thompson. The original enthusiasm for gold had subsided, although a few of the famous Overlanders continued to the diggings at William's Creek. Some went on to the coast; others settled to farm in the valleys. They had hoped to make the long trip in two months. As it was, the journey which began in June ended almost six months later, rating as one of the most adventuresome in Canadian history.

Barkerville, ultimately the terminus of the wagon road from Yale, was the undisputed capital of the gold rush by the time the Overlanders reached the end of their travels. The famous town took its name from Billy Barker, a sailor who was absent without leave from his ship on the west coast. Luck was with him, however, and after sinking a shaft on a benchland location between the creek and a steep hillside, he took gold said to have been worth half a million dollars. A town sprang up around the shaft, and it was called Barkerville.

One year after the young sailor found wealth, more than 5,000 men were working at or near the fabulous town, and fortunes were being made and lost daily. With the miners came merchants, drifters, gamblers, criminals, and dancing girls, all ready to help the miners get rid of their money. Billy Barker, according to legend, lost his half million dollars, mainly at the bars. People who were there told about a Barkerville man who entered a saloon with $50,000 in his pockets and did not leave the place until the last dollar was spent. Then, no doubt, he went back to shovelling gravel in the hope of finding more gold.

The main street of Barkerville during the days of the Gold Rush.

Government of British Columbia

One of the strangest stories from the Cariboo gold diggings concerned John A. Cameron, ultimately known as Cariboo Cameron. From his home in Glengarry, Ontario, he went to the west coast, taking his wife and infant daughter. The little girl died at Victoria, but the parents went inland where Cameron conducted a trading business and then took to mining. The first shaft in which he was interested on William's Creek yielded nothing, but the next one held a vein with a million dollars' worth of gold in it.

Then tragedy struck again. Cameron's wife died, a victim of typhoid fever. Winter was just setting in, but the sorrowing husband was determined to take the body back to Glengarry for burial. It is said that Cameron had the coffin placed in a metal box which could be sealed and instructed that it be hauled on a hand sleigh as far as Beaver Lake where a horse was obtained to pull it the rest of the way to the coast. The coffin reached Victoria in early March, more than four months after the journey was started, and there the metal container was opened, filled will alcohol, resealed, and buried.

After another summer at the mines, Cameron was ready to complete his self-assigned task, and returning to Victoria, he obtained permission to move the remains of his late wife. Accordingly, the coffin was placed on a steamer for the long trip to Montreal and then to Glengarry. There, in the Ontario community, suspicions arose. Mrs. Cameron's father wanted the coffin opened so that he might see his daughter's face again, but Cameron refused to allow it, and the body was buried again. This did not end the rumours that the coffin contained a totally different body than that of the late Mrs. Cameron. There was even some gossip about the bride who went from Glengarry having been sold to an Indian chief. Only after nine years did Cameron agree to having the casket raised for identification. Interest was intense, but when the coffin was opened, there was apparently no doubt that the remains were indeed those of Mrs. Cameron. Again the coffin was buried, but the story of Cariboo Cameron was not forgotten. As for Cameron, he lost his fortune, returned to the Cariboo to hunt for gold, and died there before he found it.

Barkerville retained its place of prominence and its salty characters for a few years, but the town, built on a single street, was never very beautiful. The big buildings, built in a hurry, were not all symmetrical nor level. Shafts in the ground could be seen everywhere, and since diggers dumped clay and tailings in the creek, the dammed-up water might leave its channel and run down the street. No one cared. Some buildings were erected on stilts, and as they settled, they seemed to slouch like carousing miners.

Freight vehicles and beasts of burden must have been about as varied as the personalities seen at Barkerville. Some of the miners walked the 600 miles from the mouth of the Fraser; some went by ship as far as Yale and walked from there or caught a ride on a freight wagon. Some of the wagons were drawn by horses, others by mules or oxen. Mule teams were favoured over horse and ox teams, but in 1862 camels made their appearance: humps, smells, sour faces, and all.

The Cariboo Trail was the only roadway in Canada on which camels were employed seriously for transportation. Frank Laumeister was credited with, or blamed for, the idea that they would travel more miles per day, carry bigger loads, and require less attention for feed and water than other draught animals. On these points, he was quite correct, but on two other counts the camels were disappointing: their relatively soft feet could not stand up to the rough and rocky roads, and furthermore, it was found almost impossible to work horse and mule outfits on the same trail as the camels.

It may have been the musky smell from the camels more than appearance that filled horses and mules with terror. A few freight shipments, one of them a cargo of rum, were lost when frightened horse and mule teams ran away, and faced with the prospect of litigation, the camel owner decided to take his imported beasts off the road. And what happened to the camels brought in to serve the gold rush? Some were sold and sent out of the country, and others of the original 23 were turned loose beside the Thompson River where they managed to survive in the wild state for a number of years.

After some more years, the lively town of Barkerville began to decay. It became a ghost town until 1958 when the province was celebrating the 100th anniversary of the birth of the Crown Colony of British Columbia, and Barkerville was marked for restoration and given the status of a park.

4 Confederation and the West

The West in Confederation Year

Confederation must be seen as a great stride in national development. In its initial stage, however, it was strictly an eastern operation. People living in the Northwest had no part in it and no particular interest. Most of them had not heard about those great struggles which were bringing four provinces into union, nor did they care.

To residents on the Atlantic side of the Great Lakes, the West of 1867 was like a foreign land, with which there was no means of direct communication except over the long canoe route finding less and less use. For western people, the lines of communication were by water through Hudson Bay to the Old Country and by cart trail to St. Paul, also known as Pig's Eye, in Minnesota.

Those who sat in the government at Ottawa had no jurisdiction in the Northwest. What is now western Canada was Rupert's Land and still in a primitive state, without settlements except at a few trading posts, without agriculture except at Red River and Fort Edmonton, without laws except those laid down by the Company, without schools except for a few at Fort Garry, without government except for the Council of Assiniboia and the fantastic "Republic of Caledonia", without means of transportation except by canoe, Red River carts, and a few steamboats on the Red, without industry or the prospect of industry except in beaver skins and buffalo robes.

The fact was that no sense of political destiny existed. The West had changed but slightly in the century after Anthony Henday trekked overland to spend a winter within sight of the Rocky Mountains, and most people in the fur trade were happy to see the country remain without change.

During the year immediately prior to Confederation, the island and mainland colonies on the Pacific side of the continent were joined to form the colony of British Columbia, an entity with an uncertain future. The gold rush was fine while it lasted, but as gold returns declined, miners went away, leaving the area which was to become the sixth province of Canada with a pronounced letdown. Something was needed to make up for the dwindling gold, and interest turned to forests and fish. The first sawmill was built on Vancouver Island in 1848, but by Confederation year, the colony had dozens of mills cutting Douglas fir, cedar, spruce, hemlock, and pine, in which the area was fabulously rich. Commercial fishing was starting in about the same way. Although coastal Indians had speared and hooked salmon and other kinds of fish for generations, Confederation year found immigrants from afar making exploratory attempts at canning on the Lower Fraser River.

What is now Alberta, Saskatchewan, and Manitoba was still the vast preserve held by the Hudson's Bay Company as an exclusive trading territory. Was it not the attraction of wild furs that led to the Company's formation in the first place, with its charter from King Charles II? For almost 200 years the Company administered the country as a piece of privately-owned real estate. When the United States purchased Alaska from Russia in 1867, paying $7,200,000 for it, the transaction suggested the possibility of the Hudson's Bay Company selling Rupert's Land to the highest bidder. As long as they owned it, however, Company men were satisfied to keep it without change.

The gold rush west of the Rockies drew public attention and thousands of fortune-seekers, but nothing of the kind had happened to change the tenor of life in the prairie area. It was, indeed, a primitive community. The first steamboats had not ventured into the North Saskatchewan River, and for anybody making the journey from Fort Garry to Fort Edmonton, the only alternative to walking was a trip by oxcart or canoe, tedious in either case.

It seems safe to presume that the Bow River country, now marked by the city of Calgary which boasts more motor vehicles per thousand of population than anywhere else in the world, had not, in Confederation year, emerged from the *travois* stage or felt the imprint on its sod of the first wheel.

A few thousand people lived in and around Fort Garry, with the French-speaking Métis outnumbering all others. A few hundred people lived in and around Fort Edmonton. Apart from these two, no settlement between the Red River and the Rockies had more than a few dozen inhabitants.

Archdeacon Cochrane went to Portage la Prairie in 1853, and Rev. James Nisbet, in 1866, led a few followers to found a community which was to become the city of Prince Albert. Métis settlements existed at places like Willow Bunch, Batoche, and Tail Creek, the latter on the north side of Red Deer River.

In what is today southern Alberta, the first white man to build a permanent habitation had not yet arrived on the scene. The whisky traders from Fort Benton, Montana, were beginning to venture as far north as the Oldman River, and in the year after Confederation, they built Fort Hamilton at a site a few miles south of the present city of Lethbridge. Although destroyed by fire in the same year, it was rebuilt on a grander scale and given the name, Whoop-Up. There the Indians were invited to trade furs and robes for a strange kind of liquor, appropriately called fire-water. Fort Whoop-Up became notorious for drunkenness and murder.

It was also in the year after Confederation that the first home was built by a white man in what is now southern Alberta. John George Brown, better known as Kootenai Brown, was the man, and his story should not be ignored. This dashing character, who became the first warden of Waterton Lakes National Park, was born in Scotland, and after his formal education at Eton and Oxford, he served in the Queen's Lifeguards. His tall and athletic figure carried a uniform well, and with bearskin busby on his head, he was a commanding-looking officer. Even the ladies in the royal household could not hide their interest, and superior officers thought it best to post him to India, a safe distance away. There, according to stories, somebody was shot, and John George Brown showed an immediate interest in seeing South America.

Before long, Brown was making his way northward, passing Panama, and joining the 49ers going on to the California gold fields. From there, Brown hunted, traded, and quarrelled with western Indians, ultimately arriving in British Columbia with a band of irritated Indians in hot pursuit. With them still following him, he came through a mountain pass and looked down upon Waterton Lakes, convinced they presented the most beautiful picture he had ever seen. "When I am free of these pursuing Indians," he said to himself, "I will return and build a home beside that water."

Sure enough, with a Métis girl as his wife, he returned in 1868 to the unforgettable wonderland beside the mountains and built a log cabin, the first of its kind in a very big area. Brown became a prominent and useful citizen, cultivating some land, acting as a guide in Northwest Rebellion days, succeeding in finding the first evidence of oil in southern Alberta, and furnishing advice for cattlemen coming to establish themselves in the kingdom of range grass, where the prairies met the foothills.

The colourful Kootenai Brown, an adventurous Englishman who, after various travels and daring escapades, became the first settler in what is now southern Alberta.

Photo RCMP

A few missionaries had ventured as far as Fort Edmonton before 1867. Rev. Robert Rundle, the first Protestant missionary, was there in 1840, and Father Jean-Baptiste Thibault was sent there by the Bishop of St. Boniface in 1842. Father Albert Lacombe went to Fort Edmonton in 1852, and Rev. John McDougall followed in 1862. In Confederation year, however, it would have been impossible to find a doctor, dentist, fireman, or policeman in a million square miles of country west and northwest from Fort Garry.

When an aching tooth tormented Rev. John McDougall, and there was neither dentist nor dental forceps within a thousand miles, he tried to extract it with a pair of mechanic's pincers, but the tooth broke off, leaving the root to generate as much pain as ever. Only after nine years, when visiting in the East, was McDougall able to have the offending root dug out by a dentist.

The Hudson's Bay Company had attempted to discharge a duty in providing something in the nature of law and authority by setting up the Council of Assiniboia. Nevertheless, this could not be considered a democratic body, and its effectiveness was negligible except in and around Fort Garry. The judgement of Canadians of later years was that the country lacked government, and it was in an administrative vacuum that the strange thing known as the Republic of Caledonia was born.

It was the brainchild of Thomas Spence who was at Fort Garry for about a year, long enough to make himself generally unpopular, and who, in 1867, went to Portage la Prairie, where a man could be completely free to act as he pleased. Spence craved authority and Portage la Prairie offered opportunity. Therefore, at precisely the time John A. Macdonald and the other Fathers of Confederation were producing a dominion in the East, Thomas Spence was setting up his prairie republic.

Who would be the president of the republic? Naturally, the position would go to Spence. No one challenged his scheme at the outset; Spence plunged right ahead with plans. Portage la Prairie would be the capital; Spence's friends would be cabinet ministers and serve part time as constables. There was the matter of boundaries for the republic, but the president had no hesitation in fixing them: the 49th parallel would be the southern boundary, the Rocky Mountains on the west, the Arctic Circle on the north, and some unclear line on the east, this latter meaning as close to Fort Garry as Spence considered it safe to go.

Then, there had to be money for the republic, and Spence, backed by his cabinet, ruled that customs duty would be collected on all goods coming into the republic and all goods going out. Apparently, officers appointed by Spence did manage to collect some duty money, and he was able to maintain a perfect balance of budget. The secret formula was simple enough: all income was spent on whisky for the president and members of his cabinet, and there was neither surplus nor deficit.

Everything was going fine for a while; however, it seems to be the fate of potentates and autocrats that sooner or later they make the errors which are their downfall. Spence's mistake was in picking a quarrel with a MacPherson. This Scot, a shoemaker living at High Bluff, not far east of Portage la Prairie, took a contemptuous view of the republic. What he had to say about the necessity of paying duty taxes to a republic which did not really exist reached the ears of the president. An order went out for MacPherson's arrest on a charge of treason.

It was wintertime and snow was deep on the Portage Plains. Two of the republic's constables drove out to High Bluff to bring the alleged criminal to justice, but the accused man was most uncooperative, and there was a scuffle in the snow before the officers overpowered and handcuffed him.

On their way to Portage, the police constables with MacPherson passed John McLean, first farmer on Portage Plains. Seeing his fellow Scot, McLean wanted to know what it was all about. MacPherson furnished a convincing summary and McLean's sympathies were aroused. At first McLean was going to use force to free his friend, but on further thought, he advised MacPherson to go along quietly, promising that he would be on hand at the trial in Portage that evening.

On his way to town after doing his farm chores, McLean invited two friends to accompany him. Their arrival at the place of trial coincided with the reading of the charge of treason against MacPherson. It was "treason against the laws of the republic". Seeing President Spence sitting in judgement, McLean could not hold his tongue. "What d'ye mean? Laws o' the Republic? We hae no laws and hae no Republic. Come oot o' it, ye whited sepulchre," he called defiantly. "Ye canna be baith accuser and judge."

To President Spence, it sounded like more treason, and he ordered another arrest. McLean was in no mood for more nonsense, and his fists began to fly. The table on which the lamp rested was upset, and immediately the room was in darkness. A free-for-all continued in the darkness until someone fired a revolver shot and then all was silent. After a few minutes, someone recovered the kerosene lamp and lit it. To MacPherson's surprise, the President was not to be seen.

The back of the iniquitous Republic of Portage la Prairie was broken forever, and the big country west of the Red River was still without democratic or constitutional government, a buffalo pasture waiting for men with the faith and imagination of nation-builders.

Manitoba, A Province Born in Trouble

Two years after Confederation, Prime Minister Macdonald's Government of Canada bought Rupert's Land, but not without a lot of argument and some senseless statements reflecting upon the value of the country.

People who could see no future for the West outnumbered the optimists. A century later, their derogatory words appear amusing. Had not George Simpson concluded that poverty of soil was a western handicap which would not be overcome? He was referring to country which, in 1966, produced 807 million bushels of wheat, to say nothing of many other products. And had not John Palliser seen the prairies as unsuited to settlement? Had not Sir Archibald Alison, English historian, said something about seven-eighths of British North America being "doomed to eternal sterility"? Had not Bishop Taché, in the very year after Confederation, questioned the practicability of colonizing a territory with only a few areas capable of cultivation, adding: "I acknowledge frankly that I would as soon—perhaps preferably—see the country remain as it is as see it change."

Even Sir John A. Macdonald had serious misgivings about the West, having written about this time: "I would be quite willing, personally, to leave the whole country a wilderness for the next half century, but I fear if Englishmen do not go there, Yankees will."

The Hudson's Bay Company, long the overlord in the West, was not anxious to give up its special privileges or change anything in the fur country, but its directors were wise enough to realize that some change had to come. Government leaders in London reasoned that there could be some better land use.

The Company was still the proprietor, however, and no one could deny its bargaining rights. United States interests were ready to discuss purchasing the entire territory. It is believed that American financiers went as far as to make an offer for Rupert's Land and their proposition was considered carefully. Moreover, there were those people in the West, especially among the Red River Métis, who were favourably disposed to a United States connection. Although not entirely happy about the Hudson's Bay Company trading monopoly, they would willingly have accepted a continuation of Company authority or annexation to the United States rather than any form of union with the Canadian provinces, that is, the East.

"We don't know how closely we came to losing the Northwest in 1869," a Canadian leader wrote shortly after that time.

As real estate salesmen know, the best means of stimulating a prospective purchaser's enthusiasm is by a display of interest on the part of a competing buyer. American interest had its effect, and the new Dominion government passed the Rupert's Land Act, inviting the British government to acquire the country in question "upon such terms and conditions as shall be agreed upon". The purpose of it all was to make it possible for the West to become part of Canada.

Negotiations for the surrender of the Company's territory were instituted quickly, with the understanding that the charter would have to be relinquished to the Queen before Canada could hope to gain possession. Reluctant to surrender, Company representatives asked the exorbitant price of a shilling an acre for the land, but this was rejected because it was considered far in excess of what would be obtained for it.

The purchase was finally concluded at a total price of one and one-half million dollars, plus certain small blocks of land on which Company posts stood, and one-twentieth of other lands in townships within the so-called fertile belt. The British government would advance the purchase price as a loan.

It was understood, also, that the Government of Canada, in acquiring the West, would respect all reasonable rights of both Indians and Métis living in the area. Unfortunately, before the new arrangement could be consummated, there was serious trouble at Red River, where the annexation was opposed by Louis Riel and his Métis followers who presented the Canadian government with some trying problems.

The transfer was supposed to take place on December 1, 1869. The Government of Canada had passed an act providing for temporary administration, and the Hon. William McDougall, invited to become the first Lieutenant Governor in the new order, was on his way to Fort Garry, eager to take office. Unforeseen events changed the official plans, however, and McDougall was rudely turned back as he tried to cross the border from Minnesota.

Riel's Métis people at Red River had reason for protest. They represented two-thirds of the local residents, but they had been shockingly overlooked by those who negotiated the big land deal. With Riel as their mouthpiece and leader, they were in a belligerent mood.

Whether the hostile events at Red River are described as rebellion, insurrection, or just a rough exercise in self-government, the obvious fact is that the situation was most embarrassing and explosive. No one could be sure where the responsibility belonged; indeed, there was something paradoxical about it. The action displayed by angry men could not properly be called rebellion because there was no constituted government against which to rebel. The Company had signed away its territorial claims and the Government of Canada was refusing to make payment or assume responsibility until the trouble had ended. If Riel and his followers did not have sufficient reason to govern, at least no other group could come forward with a better one.

Unrest mounted when government surveyors arrived at Red River and proceeded to run survey lines for square sections which were strange to natives accustomed to long and narrow riverlot farms. When these surveyors attempted to run lines across occupied riverlots, tempers really flared, and work was stopped abruptly by a group of French-speaking natives led by Louis Riel, the educated young Métis who gave up a training for the priesthood in order to be with his widowed mother, a daughter of the famous frontiersman, Jean-Baptiste Lagimodière. The local men promised that unless there were an immediate end to these operations, the surveying equipment would be thrown in the river, and the surveyors with it.

The work was suspended, but almost at once there was a report that McDougall had been appointed Lieutenant Governor of the new North West Territories and was already on the way to take up his duties. He intended to be at Fort Garry to assume office on December 1, the date of the transfer. Actually, he was travelling early and was at Pembina on October 30, only to be halted brutally there. Riel's men were not letting him in until they knew that the new administrative plan would be acceptable to them.

McDougall had only scorn for Riel and his fellow leaders: John Bruce, W. B. O'Donaghue, and Ambrose Lepine, and he hated to be taking orders from them. Anxious to test the Métis' determination, McDougall sent a member of his party, Captain Cameron, the son-in-law of Sir Charles Tupper, from Pembina to Fort Garry. At a barricade erected across the road a few miles south of Fort Garry, Cameron was stopped and sent back to Pembina. Restlessly and angrily, McDougall spent the winter months there beside the border, then went back to Ottawa.

On November 6, Riel took possession of Fort Garry and gradually assumed responsibility for local rule and the right to speak for the colony. Almost immediately, he issued a proclamation, inviting all communities along the river to send delegates to a meeting for the purpose of considering the best way of achieving good local government.

No one could quarrel with such a gesture, but his attitude toughened. After seizing the local newspaper, the *Nor'-Wester*, he published his own paper, the *New Nation*. Then came a 15-point bill of rights, most of the points being quite reasonable.

At the beginning of January 1870, people of the settlement met another personality whose name was to gain fame. He was Donald A. Smith, who came holding a special commission from the Government of Canada and who was there to find a solution acceptable to both sides of the dispute. An outdoor meeting was called and, on January 17, Smith faced a thousand people shivering in a temperature of 20° below zero. But his talk changed nothing.

Those who openly opposed Riel, including Hudson's Bay Company Governor William McTavish, were being rounded up and locked in the fort. It was doubtful if McTavish was strongly opposed to Riel's purpose, however, as he was a sick man at that time. When Major Boulton and about 75 volunteers marched from Portage la Prairie with the idea of releasing prisoners held at the fort, Riel's men simply arrested most of them too, Boulton included.

Riel's administration might have won lasting praise had it not been for the ill-conceived order to execute Thomas Scott. The condemned man antagonized Riel needlessly with his loud opposition and complaints, but not to the point of deserving such a penalty. He escaped after his first arrest, only to be arrested again along with Boulton's men. This time he faced a form of trial and was condemned to be shot. To the surprise of most people in the community, Riel was serious and, the next day, March 4,

1870, Scott faced a firing squad of six men. One of the riflemen was said to have taken a second shot after Scott fell to the ground.

It may be that Riel intended this as a display of firmness. If so, he made his point very clear and even refused to allow Scott's friends to claim the body. The place of burial was never revealed. Surely, it was Riel's greatest blunder and in the East, as in the West, indignation mounted. Ontario Orangemen demanded military action to suppress and punish the offenders.

In the meantime, a delegation representing Riel's provisional government was on its way to Ottawa to discuss settlement; however, eastern people were suddenly less patient. With both racial and religious differences being magnified, the basic issues became terribly confused. There was more public interest in sending an army to Red River than in gaining an understanding.

But the British North America Act of 1867 made provision for the entry of Rupert's Land and the North West Territories, and while a small army was being made ready to travel westward, legislation was being prepared for the creation of a new province. In drafting the legislation, the government accepted many of the proposals put forward by Riel's representatives, among them that the new province be called Manitoba instead of Assiniboia. The name may have been suggested in the first instance by Thomas Spence of the famous Republic of Portage la Prairie.

Only on May 11, 1870, was the Hudson's Bay Company paid for the land being surrendered but, the next day, the last day of the parliamentary session, the House of Commons passed the Manitoba Act, providing for the creation of Canada's fifth province. As originally constituted, the unit was much smaller than the province of later years and was known as the "Postage Stamp Province".

The Ottawa legislation made no immediate difference to Riel's position. He continued to exercise authority in a convincing manner, as evidenced by a loan for $15,000 received from the Hudson's Bay Company. Nevertheless, the troops which were to end his rule were on the way. The force of 1,200 men, under the command of Col. Garnet Wolseley, started in early May, travelling by the lakeboat, *Chicora*, to Port Arthur's Landing. Travel was slow and often difficult from there to Fort Garry. On August 24, Wolseley's force, with the backing and financial support of both the British and Canadian governments, arrived and marched upon the fort, hoping to take Riel by surprise. Instead of finding the leader or meeting resistance, the soldiers discovered the fort to be almost abandoned. Riel's unfinished breakfast was on the table. Along with Lepine and O'Donaghue, he had crossed the Red River to St. Boniface and, having cut the ferry cable, watched as soldiers moved in to take possession of the fort.

A few days later, a new Lieutenant Governor, Adams G. Archibald, arrived by canoe. Order was restored quickly, marking the end of the most eventful 12 months in early western history: the Canadian government's purchase of the West, the emergence of Riel's provisional government, and the creation of a province.

Peace was restored, but the Métis people were still unhappy, and it was not the last that would be heard of Riel. A short time later, he was elected to the House of Commons to represent a Manitoba constituency. When denied the right to take his seat, he ran again and was elected once more. Eastern feeling was intensely bitter against him, and after the House of Commons passed a warrant of outlawry against him, he went to the United States, where he took up residence in Montana. He was still living and teaching school there when the Saskatchewan River Métis called him back in 1884.

The New Province of British Columbia

Manitoba was born amid turmoil. British Columbia's birth a few months later was in a comparatively peaceful setting. The excitement of a gold rush had passed, leaving the colony of British Columbia slightly exhausted and moderately depressed. Among the byproduct benefits of lasting value, however, were the rugged and resourceful men who remained to build a province.

Sir James Douglas, called the "father of British Columbia", was there long before the stampede of miners and for some years after, but the rush was directly responsible for men like Judge William Begbie whose swift justice brought sober lessons to wrongdoers, Walter Moberly whose explorations revealed intermountain passes suitable for railroad construction, John Robson who became a provincial premier, and Amor de Cosmos who also served as premier and was, at the same time, one of the most colourful figures in the history of public service.

Douglas, a man of imagination and vigour, was at the peak of his influence during the years of the gold rush and retired as the tempo of mining was subsiding. Consequently, he did not have an active part in bringing British Columbia into Confederation, but it was while he served as governor that a legislative council, the forerunner to full responsible government, was constituted in the Vancouver Island colony, in 1856, the first body of its kind west of Upper Canada. Similarly, a legislative council was set up in the mainland colony in 1864. Upon retirement, Douglas made his home in Victoria and was a spectator when British Columbia followed Manitoba in taking its place as a Canadian province.

Winning support for entry into the family of Canadian provinces was not easy. As in Manitoba and the eastern provinces, there was strong opposition. A sizeable fraction of the people on the west coast favoured union with the United States.

Perhaps the most effective backing for provincial status came from John Robson and Amor de Cosmos. Although rivals in occupation, their records were strikingly similar. Both were newspaper editors, both were untiring fighters for anything in which they believed, and both attained the high office of Premier of British Columbia.

Robson, an Ontario man, came to the West in 1859 and was in on the rewarding gold mining at Hill's Bar, just below Yale. Two years later, he started a newspaper at New Westminster, becoming a power in guiding public opinion. When the capital of the United Colony of British Columbia was moved from New Westminster to Victoria in 1868, Robson also moved, but he returned in a few years to the mainland centre he had helped to lay out and build. In time he was elected to the provincial legislature, still speaking and writing boldly about provincial rights. In 1889, Robson became premier.

Amor de Cosmos was a picturesque gentleman, tall, dark, and striking in appearance, looking the part of a storybook villain more than a struggling newspaperman. He was born at Windsor, Nova Scotia, and given the undistinctive name of Alexander Smith. But there was nothing commonplace about this man. Seeking adventure, he went to California and, while there, succeeded in obtaining an act of the state legislature to change his name legally to Amor de Cosmos, meaning "lover of the world".

Using his new name, he was at Victoria with the first wave of gold seekers, but instead of following the river gravels, he remained at Victoria and started a newspaper, the *Colonist*. The first issue appeared on December 11, 1858, carrying an attack upon the autocratic ways of Governor Douglas. The editor wrote boldly and well, supporting responsible government, the union of the two colonies, and later, British Columbia's entry into federation.

After becoming a member of the colony's Legislative Council, de Cosmos was more pro-federationist than ever, and on March 10, 1867, Confederation year, he made an historic motion calling for British Columbia to join with the eastern provinces in forming the new Dominion of Canada. The motion did not carry, but it did help to counteract the rising demand for annexation to the United States. Alaska, through purchase, became United States property and, with many American miners remaining in the country after the gold rush, it was not surprising to find a desire to give the United States an unbroken shoreline all the way to the Arctic.

Those people favouring union with the United States advanced some rather practical reasons: California offered the best market for what British Columbia had to sell, and San Francisco, with which there was regular boat service, seemed less remote than Ottawa or Montreal. Even the ships which carried most of the British Columbia mail, both in and out, flew U.S. flags.

An annexationist society was formed and gaining strength, but de Cosmos was not asleep. With him as instigator, a confederation league was organized and it, too, was popular. Clearly, the lines were being drawn for a fine political fight.

Even within the Legislative Council, there was division, with Governor Seymour and most of his appointed members opposing union with Canada. When a proposal for such union came before the council in December 1868, it was turned down. The anti-federationists in the council at that time had a majority of the votes, but the federationists had the most vigorous leaders and soon saw the winds of politics changing in their favour.

In 1869, when the Government of Canada and the Hudson's Bay Company were coming to terms for the transfer of Rupert's Land, Governor Seymour died and was succeeded by Anthony Musgrave, formerly the Governor of Newfoundland, who proved to be a strong advocate of British Columbia's entry into the family of Canadian provinces. Under his influence, the British Columbia Executive Council came to favour confederation. Amor de Cosmos had the backing he needed, and sentiment was changing to his fancy. The question of union dominated the council debates in 1870, and three delegates were named to proceed to Ottawa in order to discuss terms of entry.

De Cosmos was not one of the delegates, but he was a personal friend of Sir John A. Macdonald and had no trouble in gaining the Prime Minister's favour for the idea. The negotiations led to agreement: the Dominion would assume the colony's debt, make an annual grant of 80 cents per person, and build a railroad between East and West within 10 years. It has been said that the delegates went to Ottawa prepared to settle for a wagon road but that Macdonald offered the bigger prize of a railroad.

In due course, the terms were ratified by the Legislative Council and the House of Commons and, on July 20, 1871, British Columbia became Canada's sixth province. It was to have a legislative assembly like that of Ontario, and J. F. McCreight became the province's first premier, followed by Amor de Cosmos.

5 The Law on Horseback

The Mounties Ride West

When the West became part of Canada, something in the way of law enforcement was urgently necessary. William Francis Butler said so officially in 1871, and Colonel Robertson Ross repeated it in 1872.

Butler was the young Irishman who came with the Wolseley expedition and then accepted a commission from the new Lieutenant Governor of Manitoba and the Territories to report on what would be necessary for maintaining peace and order. Butler wrote:

> "The institutions of Law and Order, as understood in civilized communities, are wholly unknown in the regions of the Saskatchewan, insomuch as the country is without any executive organization, and destitute of any means to enforce the authority of the law. . . . It is an undoubted fact that crimes of the most serious nature have been committed . . . without any vindication of the law being possible. . . ."
>
> WILLIAM FRANCIS BUTLER, *The Great Lone Land*,
> Sampson Low, Marston, Low, and Searle, London, 1872.

Butler said that what was needed was a police force of from 100 to 150, one-third of them mounted. Col. Robertson Ross reported that white settlers were in danger and hardly dared to introduce cattle. He recommended a mounted constabulary.

Nobody could ignore the danger of Indian uprisings accompanied by terrible slaughter. The way native people engaged in intertribal warfare showed how lightly they regarded killing. The last of the major Indian battles, between the traditional enemies, Crees and Blackfoot, took place in 1870. A cairn on the outskirts of Lethbridge marks the place.

An account of that battle, written by Dr. G. A. Kennedy while memory of it was still fresh in the minds of men who had witnessed it, was published in the *Lethbridge News* of April 30, 1890. Some famous chiefs took part, but the hero of the day was Jerry Potts, the little Métis whose later associations with the Mounted Police brought him fame.

About 600 to 800 Crees followed Chiefs Piapot, Big Bear, and Little Pine and waited at the Oldman River for an opportunity to strike for enemy scalps. But before they realized it, they were in trouble. War-whoops echoed through the river valley as Bloods, Blackfoot and, finally, Piegans came eager for battle. The outnumbered Crees withdrew to more favourable fighting locations in river coulees, about where the high level railway bridge was built later. At an opportune moment, Jerry Potts called for an attack which forced Crees into the flooded river where they continued to come under fire from enemy guns and bows. Only a remnant of the defeated Crees returned to home camps in what is now Saskatchewan.

In arousing Canadians to the urgency of the need, neither reports from experts like Butler and Ross nor stories of Indian wars did as much as the Cypress Hills Massacre. Accounts differed on how it was carried out, but there was agreement on one point: the mass killing of Indians in the Cypress Hills on a May day in 1873 was both senseless and savage. The fact that it was carried out by so-called civilized whites made it seem all the worse. Before the end of that year, the North West Mounted Police force was authorized, and recruiting was well under way.

The shameful massacre had a background in whisky trading and horse stealing, both too common at the time. White traders from Fort Benton, Montana, were responsible for sale of the firewater brand of liquor and Indians for most of the horse stealing. Indian thieving forays were usually directed at enemy tribesmen, but they did not hesitate to gather a band of good horses owned by a trader or settler, or even a police force.

As it happened on this occasion, a band of Canadian Crees rode south for the express purpose of taking horses from their Montana Blackfoot enemies. Before reaching the Blackfoot camp, however, they came upon an unguarded band of horses owned by traders from Fort Benton. The temptation was overwhelming, and the Canadian Crees turned toward home with the white men's horses.

It was not the first time these traders had lost horses, and they vowed to punish the offenders. Back at Fort Benton, they secured aid from friends, and 13 men with fresh horses and breech-loading rifles rode out to recover the horses and punish the thieves. Returning to the place where the stolen horses were last seen, the Benton men were able to follow tracks for some miles. Then, having lost the tracks, they simply rode on across the border and into the Cypress Hills where they camped beside Battle Creek, close to a trading post conducted by Abel Farwell. The exact location would be about four miles downstream from the point at which the Mounted Police built Fort Walsh a few years later.

By this time, the traders had no idea where either the lost horses or the thieves might be, but after celebrating with a keg of rum, they were ready to take revenge against any Indians in sight. Abel Farwell, who gave evidence at a trial in Winnipeg, attempted to convince the men from Benton that Assiniboine Indians occupying about 40 lodges just across the creek were not the horse thieves. Thomas Hardwick and other traders did not seem to care. If these Indians did not steal the traders' horses, they probably stole other horses. The Montana men wanted to kill Indians, and at daybreak, after a night of drinking and boasting, 16 white men with loaded guns advanced upon the Indian camp. In a matter of minutes, 100 shots were fired and at least 20 Indians were dead or dying. Only one of the attackers, Ed Grace, fell in the shooting.

Not satisfied after shooting every Indian in sight, the white men rushed the camp, rolled the tipis together, and set them on fire. The men from the south contended that Indians fired the first shot, but Farwell denied it.

News of the crime was slow in reaching Fort Garry and the East. Sir John A. Macdonald's government ordered steps to have the offenders brought from Montana to face charges. That was not an easy order for Canadian authorities to carry out and not much happened, at least, not until after the Mounted Police arrived to build Fort Macleod late in the next year. Among those who went to Montana to secure United States release of the accused men was Col. Macleod of the force. Washington officials were cooperative, but local feeling at Fort Benton was strongly with the accused men and Macleod faced impossible odds. Montana people were not ready to let any of their citizens be taken to another country for trial and, perhaps, hanging, just for killing a few Indians. Not only were the accused men released for lack of evidence, but a counter charge was laid against Col. Macleod, and he experienced the indignity of a brief spell in a Fort Benton jail. Three of the accused men were later arrested on the Canadian side and taken to Winnipeg for trial; however, by that time the evidence was more fragmentary, and the charges were dismissed.

The only good thing to come from the shameful event was a Canadian determination that no such atrocity would ever again be allowed to happen on Canadian soil. Under the guiding hand of Sir John A. Macdonald, the Parliament of Canada, on May 23, 1873, passed an act providing for the North West Mounted Police. It was to be a force under civil authority but with military discipline. To the neighbouring United States, removed by nothing more than a thin boundary line, the term "Mounted Police" was thought to be less offensive than "Mounted Rifles".

Recruiting began without delay. To qualify, a man would have to be "of sound constitution, able to ride, active and able-bodied, of good character and between the ages of 18 and 40 and able to read and write in French or English". A constable's pay would be $1.00 per day, and upon completion of a term of three years in service and an honourable discharge, he could claim a free grant of one quarter section of land.

The first group of 150 police recruits went over the Dawson Route to Red River before the end of the year, and on June 6, 1874, the main body, comprising 16 officers, 200 men, and 244 horses, left Toronto to travel through United States territory to the end of the railroad at Fargo, North Dakota. From Fargo, officers and men travelled by trail to Fort Dufferin in southern Manitoba, where they met up with the group which wintered at Fort Garry and prepared for the long trek to some uncertain point near the Rockies.

Under the command of Commissioner G. A. French and Assistant Commissioner James F. Macleod, the great police cavalcade began its notable march on July 8. It must have presented a rare picture: 114 Red River carts loaded with supplies, 73 wagons, agricultural implements, 142 work oxen, 93 other cattle, and 310 horses. The column was orderly as well as big, even to the grouping of horses according to colours. Divisions A had all dark bay horses; Division B, dark browns; Division C, light chestnuts; Division D, greys and buckskins; and Division E, blacks. Apart from a few Indians, no spectators were present to enjoy the parade, which was at least a couple of miles long.

At La Roche Percée, on July 29, Inspector W. D. Jarvis and A Troop separated and followed the trail to Fort Ellis and Fort Edmonton, a journey not completed until November 1. The main body continued westward, making its own trail much of the time. Hardships increased; a few men deserted, and many horses and oxen died along the way. The police officers, who were strangers on the prairies, did not know exactly where they were going. French and Macleod returned from a side trip to Fort Benton with fresh horses and an incomparable Métis guide, Jerry Potts. This son of a Scottish trader father and Piegan Indian mother became the eyes, ears, and nose of the force. With many of the instincts of a homing pigeon, he was never lost. When water was scarce, little Jerry could direct the thirsty force to a spring. Best of all, this man who was half-Indian and half-white was able to command the respect of both races. In that alone, he was able to contribute much to the success of the police.

Jerry Potts, soon after coming with the force, directed it to Fort Whoop-Up where the police expected to have a fight on their hands. As it was, the famous and iniquitous fort was almost abandoned, and the officers considered trying to buy it for a headquarters site. The price suggested seemed ridiculously high, however, and the police continued on until October 13, when a halt was called at a spot on the Oldman River to which Jerry Potts had guided them.

There the officers decided to build a fort, and the far-western post to be known as Fort Macleod was ready for occupation before Christmas. Other posts were established within the next year. Inspector Jarvis, who had taken the trail to Edmonton, built at Fort Saskatchewan. Fort Walsh in the Cypress Hills and Fort Calgary on the Bow River were also built in 1875.

Wherever they built, the police had many obstacles to overcome before winning the confidence of the Indians which was greatly needed if order were to be established on the broad face of the West. The whisky trade carried on by men from the south was rather quickly halted, and although horse stealing and cattle rustling were never completely eliminated, they were checked.

One of the first visitors at the new post on Oldman River was Chief Crowfoot, who came simply to find out what he could about police purposes. Col. Macleod received him and undertook to explain that anybody who avoided wrongdoing had nothing to fear from men in police uniform. The police were there to protect Indians as much as whites, and Crowfoot was impressed. If that were the way police worked, he would help them.

Many stories have been told to illustrate the favourable relationship established between the Indians and police. One of them, told with some variations, concerned the band of disgruntled Crees which fled to the United States in the hope of finding better hunting. The American authorities did not want another cattle-killing band and asked the Canadian government to take its Indians home. Canadian authorities agreed to take them, provided that the Americans would deliver the Indians at the border.

United States cavalry units were given the chore of rounding up the unhappy Canadian Indians and practically herding them to the international boundary. There, to the surprise of the American army men, a Canadian mounted policeman, Constable Daniel Davis, better known as "Peaches" Davis, stood alone.

"Where are your men to take charge of these Indians?" the United States officer asked, and Davis replied: "I'm taking them."

The Americans watched with amazement, as the Canadian Mountie, supported by wagons loaded with rations, moved away in the general direction of Battleford.

In 1904, the North West Mounted Police became the Royal North West Mounted Police by royal proclamation, and after World War I, the Royal

Canadian Mounted Police. The new name did not change the ideals and standard of service, and Canadians had reason for pride. Frontier service extended far beyond law enforcement. The police engaged in some farming and were often the means of encouraging agriculture. They conducted the first mail service in what is now southern Alberta, and they rendered valuable assistance during the construction of the Canadian Pacific Railway and the troubled times of 1885.

One way or another, they built a proud record of achievement. Through the exercise of patience, impartiality, and firmness, they won the Indians and won even international admiration.

1876 — A Year To Be Remembered

For students of western history, 1876 was a year to be remembered. South of the border, it was the year of the Custer Massacre at Little Big Horn, Montana, where Sitting Bull's troubled Sioux Indians completely wiped out a force of United States cavalry under General George Custer. Fear of vengeance then brought the Sioux war chief and a few thousand of his followers to the Canadian prairies, where they posed serious problems until persuaded to return to the United States.

Less sensational but more significant was the fact that the year brought the clearest evidence that wheat and cattle would become important items of production. The first wheat was shipped from the West, the first cattle were marketed from British Columbia, and the first cattle were turned out to winter on grassland in what is now Alberta.

The valley ranges between the mountains had cattle for some years before the first herds were released on the shortgrass plains. The gold rush in the Cariboo provided the reasons, for the thousands of miners who flocked to the British Columbia interior had to be fed, and there were those astute cattlemen who sensed more reward in furnishing beef than in digging for gold. Among them were Jerome and Thaddeus Harper who, in 1862, drove a herd of several hundred cattle from Oregon. The route was dotted with obstacles like mountains, canyons, and swift rivers, but the Harpers succeeded in completing delivery, and beef selling at 75 cents a pound was sufficient to send the cattlemen back to Oregon for another herd. In 1864, they delivered the third herd in three years, but by this time miners were leaving the Cariboo, and the market for beef was seriously depressed. The Harper cattle had practically no value in the Fraser River country, and they were certainly not worth driving back to Oregon.

What was to be done? Instead of abandoning the third herd, the Harper brothers branded the cattle and turned them out to graze and enjoy the freedom of unoccupied country. The result was exactly as might have been expected: the cows had calves, and in time, the calves grew up and they had calves. The herd was becoming big, and friends laughed at the apparent folly of rounding up and branding cattle for which there was no market and no prospect of a market.

The herd had become imposingly large. Jerome Harper died and Thaddeus had full responsibility. Somebody reminded Thaddeus that he was wasting his time, adding: "There's no railway to carry cattle and, even if there were a railway, there's no market nearer than Chicago."

Harper replied: "There's an idea. Chicago! How would a man driving a herd of cattle get there?"

The friend could not tell Harper how to get there, but Harper said he was sure he could find it and would report when he returned.

With good horses and riders, Harper rounded up 800 head of his cattle, all about as wild as the moose and deer with which they had been sharing the intermountain grazing, and drove them southward, past Fort Kamloops, along the west side of Okanagan Lake and into United States territory. Now Harper and his helpers were in country where cattle were being kept and, suddenly, the herd grew from 800 head to 1,200. The increase in numbers was not explained.

Day after day, the cattlemen added 12 or 15 miles to the distance travelled. They drove across the state of Washington, across Oregon, across Idaho, and were part way across Utah when winter overtook them. Harper's decision was to camp there until spring. At this point, a traveller driving a team of mules came in from the west and, after chatting with Harper, remarked: "You know, I believe your critters would be worth more at San Francisco than at Chicago."

Here was an idea that Harper had not considered but he replied at once: "Do you think so? Then, we'll go to San Francisco."

When spring came, the big herd was headed to the southwest and driven over more rocky passes, across more ferocious rivers, and through more

Photo MacEwan

The original Harper buildings, where the Harper brothers began ranching on the South Thompson River in British Columbia.

Indian country, all strange and new to the men. Some 18 months after leaving his British Columbia range, Harper drove the big herd into San Francisco and sold it at prices that made the whole venture seem worthwhile. He then returned to raise more cattle in his intermountain pastures, where other cattlemen like Joe Greaves, who founded the Douglas Lake Ranch, were picking up the idea of ranching on the broad valleylands.

On the shortgrass plains east of the Rockies, the situation was quite different. There had been no gold rush mobs to be fed, and nobody was eager to introduce cattle while buffalo herds were still numerous, and no-madic Indians would as soon shoot a steer as a buffalo. Although those grassy plains ultimately gained very high favour for ranching purposes, the first big herds did not reach there until six or seven years after Manitoba and British Columbia were created as provinces.

Two years after the Mounted Police built Fort Macleod, John B. Smith of Sun River, Montana, drove 14 cows, 10 calves, and a bull to Fort Macleod, presumably to sell them. Surely he did not expect to sell them to a mounted policeman but, whether through purchase or the circumstances of a poker game, the cattle came into the hands of a Constable Whitney. Regardless of whether or not he wanted the cattle, Whitney had no way of taking care of them, no stable accommodation and no winter feed. What was he to do with the herd? To leave them out all winter seemed foolhardy because, as friends were ready to point out, the cattle would freeze to death or drift away with the big migrating herds of buffalo, ending up in Kansas.

Whitney had no choice and simply turned the herd loose where domestic cattle had never roamed before. He tried to forget about his animals for the winter months, but with the return of spring, he felt curious to know what had happened. He rode out from the fort, hoping to find some trace of the animals or their remains. He was not at all hopeful of finding them alive, but to everybody's surprise, after an absence of a couple of days he returned, driving his 25 cattle. Every cow had a calf, and Whitney's herd was signalling the beginning of cattle ranching on that side of the mountains. Nevertheless, the real lifeblood for the new West was not beef but wheat, and what happened at Winnipeg in 1876 deserves to be remembered annually on October 21.

Settlers beside the Red River and farther west had been growing wheat in a most indifferent way, strictly for local use. Sometimes the crop yielded well, while sometimes, as in the grasshopper years of the early seventies, wheat was a failure. Without a practical means of transportation to the East, there was not much incentive to produce more than a small western population could consume.

It came as a complete surprise in the autumn of 1876 to hear of a Toronto man being in the Red River community, prepared, of all things, to pay 80 cents a bushel in cash for wheat to be sent to the East. Ontario had a poor crop that year, and the seed firm of Steele Brothers was hard pressed to find supplies for its trade. Having heard about a good crop being harvested in Manitoba, R. C. Steele, junior member of the Toronto firm, resolved to make the long trip. The easiest way of getting to Winnipeg was to travel by rail as far as Fisher's Landing in Minnesota, then to switch to Red River steamboat for the last part of the journey. Accordingly, young Steele took the train to the rail terminal north of St. Paul but, instead of waiting for a slow riverboat, he saved valuable time by hiring a team and wagon and driving to Winnipeg. Time was valuable because he hoped to buy wheat early enough so that it could be shipped out by boat before the Red River froze over in the late autumn.

At journey's end, Steele met David Young of the local firm of Higgins and Young, "Dealers in Boots and Shoes, Crockery and Glassware", and invited assistance in buying 5,000 bushels of Manitoba wheat. For a week after October 13, the *Manitoba Daily Free Press* carried the announcement: "Cash for choice wheat to export to Ontario". Higgins and Young, as purchasing agents, were to receive 5 cents per bushel, making the total cost to Steele Brothers of 85 cents per bushel, plus 35 cents per bushel for freight and 26 cents each for the necessary cotton bags.

Anyway, the response was immediate. Farmers near and far prepared to sack and deliver all the wheat they could spare. Nothing like this had ever happened before, and carts converged upon McMillan's Mill, close to the Red River, where delivery was to be made. The biggest single transaction involved 204 bushels delivered by G. R. Miller of Kildonan.

The most significant point about the shipment was that Steele failed to obtain the 5,000 bushels he wanted. The fact of the matter was that the West of 1876, nine years after Confederation, did not have that much. After buying all the available wheat, the Toronto man had 857 bushels and 10 pounds. The grain was tied securely in 412 new bags and piled on the sternwheeler, *Selkirk*, to be taken upstream on the Red, overland to Duluth, by lakeboat to Sarnia, and by rail to Toronto.

This was Red Fife wheat, a completely new variety at Red River, where it had been introduced following loss of seed due to grasshoppers in the previous couple of years. Strangely enough, this new wheat, which showed a special fondness for western soil, was Canadian in origin, having taken its name from David Fife, a Scottish settler at Peterborough, Ontario. The Toronto grain merchants and dealers in seed had seen Red Fife wheat before, but never had they seen anything quite like this, and they wanted more of the same. They enquired how they could obtain more. The answer should have been obvious: by building a railroad to connect with the West where wheat-producing soil was waiting for men to cultivate it.

The little trickle represented by 857 bushels and 10 pounds of wheat shipped out in 1876 was soon to become a torrent of bread wheat measured in many millions of bushels. While Canadians celebrated the 90th anniversary of that first shipment of wheat from the West, they were being informed that the current year's production from western soil was 807 million bushels.

Blackfoot Treaty Number Seven

There was no doubt about it: the uncertainty of Indian temper in the southwestern section of the prairies was enough to discourage traders and settlers from going there. Members of the Blackfoot, Blood, Piegan, Sarcee, and Stoney tribes were known to be cranky and tough. Naturally, they resented the new order and did not hesitate to display their anger. As a result, the acceptance of a settlement treaty on September 22, 1877, was seen as a major triumph in taming the West.

By the terms of the British North America Act of 1867, "Indians and lands reserved for Indians" were to be the responsibility of the Government of Canada, and in the four decades following, ten separate treaties were drawn up and signed with tribal groups in western and central Canada. Seven of those were signed during the seventies.

Treaties One and Two, involving Manitoba Indians, were executed in 1871, and new ones were signed at the rate of one per year from 1873 to 1876. But the problem of getting agreement from the Blackfoot and their neighbours was viewed with apprehension. Buffalo herds were in decline, adding to Indian fear and anger at the new situation in the West. There could be no hope of success for homesteading or ranching in those parts until Indians had accepted treaty terms and reservations. Even the building of a railroad across the plains would have been to court danger. To obtain agreement for a treaty with these, the most difficult of all the native people, would be a climactic event indeed.

For the Hon. David Laird, Lieutenant Governor of the North West Territories, and Commissioner James Macleod of the Mounted Police, named to negotiate with the Indians and sign on behalf of the government, the task must have seemed rather fearsome.

Having received his instructions from Ottawa, Laird left the territorial capital at Fort Livingstone on August 11, 1877. After 24 days on the trail, he and his party reached Fort Macleod where the meeting with Indians of five tribes was supposed to take place. Unfortunately, those planning the meeting had forgotten to consult with the "Chief of Chiefs", the influential Crowfoot of the Blackfoot. He had his own opinions on most subjects, and on this one, he insisted that the meeting be at Blackfoot

Crossing on the Bow River, below Fort Calgary. The government men had the good sense to make the change without argument.

Today a cairn overlooking the river marks the place of meeting and signing of Treaty Number Seven. The location, south of Cluny, is one of beauty, and for generations, it was a favoured camping site with prairie Indians. Being at the very heart of good buffalo country gave it added attraction.

Monday, September 17, was the day set for the meeting. Commissioner Macleod, riding with 80 of his officers and men of the still youthful force, arrived a few days in advance, and the Lieutenant Governor arrived with one day to spare. By this time, the landscape was dotted with Blackfoot and Stoney tipis, and smoke from hundreds of campfires filled the valley.

Bloods, Piegans, and Sarcees, never much impressed by the white man's slavish adherence to clock and calendar, were late in arriving, and the Monday meeting was postponed to Wednesday. The Indians did not care, however, because the government was prepared to issue rations of beef, flour, tea, sugar, and tobacco, and most of the native people were eating better than usual. The majority accepted the government gifts of food, but not the great and noble Crowfoot. Nobody would be able to say that he had been bribed or influenced by gifts of any kind.

In the meantime, Indians at the site were given an opportunity to become familiar with the proposed terms in advance of the general assembly. Thus, they would be able to discuss them around the campfires.

As suggested, there would be reservations, annual payments in cash, later known as "treaty money", assistance in getting started with cattle, and farm implements and gifts of ammunition for hunting. That part sounded all right, but there was that other part: every native would find it painful to give up his traditional freedoms and surrender inherited rights on 50,000 square miles of prairie territory.

As the time set for the big meeting drew near, young Blackfoot braves staged demonstrations which no one among the spectators would soon forget. Several hundreds of them, mounted, painted, and frightening with their war-whoops, raced their horses back and forth on the campground. As they galloped madly, they fired muzzle-loaders in the air. Mounted police, with carbines at their sides, stood motionless and silent. Observers had reasons for being worried. Richard Hardisty speculated that if there had been any indication of fear or an accidental discharge of a police rifle, a battle resulting in terrible slaughter might have erupted.

The exact reason for the display was not clear, but Crowfoot, remaining calm, walked to the commissioners, lit his long-stemmed pipe, and took the first puff. He then passed the pipe, in turn, to the Lieutenant Governor and the Commissioner of the Mounted Police.

The assembly was a big one, probably the biggest gathering of Indians the country had seen. Seated in front were the head chiefs, while more than 4,000 other Indians stood or squatted behind them.

After some explanations about the proposed treaty, the meeting was adjourned to allow the chiefs to conduct further discussions among themselves. When Crowfoot indicated a willingness to resume with the main meeting, he came forward and was the first to speak. His leadership was acknowledged, and other Indians were likely to accept his views.

Addressing the two government representatives, he said: "This has been our home. The buffalo have always been our food. I hope you will look upon the Blackfoot, Bloods, Piegans, and Sarcees as your children now and that you will be considerate and charitable to them. They all expect me to speak for them and I trust the Great Spirit will put into their breasts to be good people, also into the minds of men, women and children of future generations."

He was speaking like an elder statesman as he continued:

"The advice given to me and my people has proven to be good. If the police had not come to this country, where would we all be now? Bad men and whisky were killing us so fast that very few of us would have been alive today. The Mounted Police protected us as the feathers of the bird protect it from frosts of winter. I wish all my people good and trust that all our hearts will increase in goodness from this time forward. I am satisfied. I will sign the treaty."

Yes, Crowfoot would sign; he would be the first to sign, and the last to break a promise.

Eagle Tail spoke for the Piegans, Bearspaw for the Stonies, Bull's Head for the Sarcees, and Rainy Chief for the North Bloods. Red Crow of the South Bloods arrived the following day, but he also agreed, and then there was the formal signing, commissioners signing first and then the chiefs, in turn, adding their marks.

There were special gifts of flags, uniforms, and medals for the chiefs, and then some feasting and a lot of chanting. Young braves continued what looked terrifyingly like battle exercises, galloping through the valley, shrieking, and firing their guns toward the sky. It was difficult to know how much of this was inspired by approval and how much by disapproval and hostility; however, the demonstrations ended and there were discussions about reserves. The authorities and the Indians were not in complete agreement about locations for reservations.

Finally, there was the most popular part of the program, the payment of treaty money: $25 to each of 10 chiefs, $15 to each of 40 minor chiefs and councillors, and $1 each to 4,342 men, women, and children. Altogether, $52,954 was the sum paid to 4,392 Indians of five tribes.

Crowfoot, chief of the Black-foot tribe, was the most influen-tial and respected Indian of his time.

Glenbow Foundation

The big show ended, and after the government rations ran out, the Indians went their various ways. Commissioner Macleod returned to his post on the Oldman River, and Lieutenant Governor Laird set out for Battleford, chosen to be the new capital of the North West Territories.

6 The Railways and the Land Rush

The Achievement of a Railroad

An ocean-to-ocean concept of Canadian development called for something better than canoe routes and cart trails to link the East and West. Improved transportation facilities seemed to be an essential ingredient for the success of Confederation. Clearly, the prospect of a railroad to be started "within six months after Union" was an important inducement in bringing the Maritime areas into Confederation and the intercolonial railway was one of the first Confederation promises to be fulfilled.

More important and more gigantic was the proposed transcontinental railway, a dream to be realized only after loud political controversy, near-ruinous financial difficulties, and what seemed like almost insurmountable technical problems. It is significant that the plan which meant so much to the West was carried through. After defying the barriers of geography, the new railroad spanning the continent stood as an engineering and political achievement commanding admiration from many parts of the world.

Some Easterners, afraid of cost, scoffed at the idea of a railway reaching to the Pacific. It would be uneconomic, they were sure, and the builders would suffer bankruptcy. As an investment, it would never pay interest on the axle grease. If more reasons for opposition were needed, the forbidding mountain barriers would surely supply them. It would have been more sensible, according to some voices of the time, to settle for a wagon road to the Pacific.

Among those who believed a railway from Atlantic to Pacific could and should be built was Sir John A. Macdonald, who promised the people of British Columbia they would have rails within 10 years after joining as a province in 1871. In fulfilling the agreement, construction ran far behind schedule, and residents on the west coast became impatient and talked about secession to the United States.

It was up to the Government of Canada to convince the people of the East that the West was worth a railroad. Even Macdonald, as Prime Minister, had shown doubt, but when committed to the undertaking, he accepted the transcontinental challenge with typical determination. He hoped the costly railroad would be undertaken by private capitalists.

Two rival groups were interested in building, and until after the federal election of 1872, Sir John encouraged both, no doubt hoping that the two companies would amalgamate for the mammoth undertaking. Early in 1873, however, the government granted an exclusive charter to the group headed by Sir Hugh Allan and at once incurred the criticism of the rival bidders for the privilege. Charges were made that Macdonald had been aided in his election campaign with contributions from Sir Hugh Allan, and the so-called Pacific Scandal resulted.

The Opposition in the House of Commons made the most of circumstances, and the Governor General wrote to Macdonald, noting that his "personal honour is as stainless as it has ever been", but advising resignation. In November 1873, the Macdonald government resigned, and the Liberals under the leadership of Alexander Mackenzie took office and reassessed the railroad situation. A more cautious leader, Mackenzie favoured a government-built communication, partly rail, partly water. It would cost less and could be built one stage at a time, as funds became available.

How would Canada have developed if Mackenzie's policies had been carried out? It is a good question for contemplation. Settlement of the West would have been slower, but the large amount of land granted to the railway builders might have been retained or used to better public advantage.

Mackenzie's plan sounded fair enough at the time, but it was not enough to keep Macdonald as the Opposition. In the election of 1878, Macdonald was returned to power with fresh vigour for the construction of an unbroken rail connection between the Atlantic and Pacific. In wanting the road to be built by private capital, Sir John's ideas were unchanged, even though he would be prepared to offer inducements and even financial help.

A few politicians found support for their continuing resistance to government subsidies in any form, as shown by one who drew cheers at a Nova Scotia meeting in 1879 when he proclaimed: "We will never allow public funds to be spent for rails across the rocks and muskeg of Western Ontario, the waste spaces of the prairies, and the useless valleys of British Columbia."

In spite of opposition, rails reached Winnipeg from the East in 1879 and a local real estate boom followed at once. Where the line would go from there and who would build it were still very much in doubt.

Sandford Fleming's recommendation was for a route touching Battleford and Fort Edmonton and traversing the Rockies by the Yellowhead Pass. Thus, the railroad would serve Palliser's fertile belt and have the added benefit of a relatively favourable grade in mountain country. The highest point would be 3,717 feet above sea level, considerably lower than the mile-high height of the land on the Kicking Horse route.

After long debate, a new railroad plan was approved in February 1881, granting the charter to a syndicate, later known as the Canadian Pacific Railway. The syndicate drove a hard bargain and was granted 25,000,000 acres of western land, $25,000,000 in cash, and a big measure of railway monopoly. Almost at once, the route to be taken across the West was changed. A fear had grown that if a railway were not built across the southern prairies, United States railways, expanding rapidly, would attract too much Canadian trade. At the same time, it did not seem desirable from the viewpoint of national defence to have the railroad very close to the international boundary. Government approval was granted for a change of route, provided that the railroad, in crossing the plains, was kept beyond 100 miles from the border. Instead of taking the northwesterly course by way of Fort Edmonton, the railroad would now be built more directly westward from Winnipeg, touching Portage la Prairie and Fort Calgary and negotiating the mountains by the Kicking Horse Pass. Construction westward from Winnipeg began in 1881, and by the next year, the syndicate was organized for faster operations in building grades and laying tracks. William Van Horne, as General Manager, brought new drive to the construction, but there were still many problems, some financial, some engineering, some Indian. Chief Piapot and his unhappy Crees protested in the only way they knew. Objecting to the prospect of locomotives belching smoke back and forth and frightening game, they pulled up the wood survey stakes and used them for campfires. When this did not stop Van Horne's crews, the natives simply pitched their tipis on the right of way, just ahead of the workers, and refused to move. Labourers had no desire to quarrel with these well-armed Indians and appealed to the Mounted Police who proved to be more persuasive than the engineers.

Even more serious were the financial problems. In desperation, the syndicate appealed to the government which, reluctantly, loaned $22,-500,000 in 1883 and $5,000,000 in 1884. Even though the company was considered a poor risk at that time, the government could not afford to let the railway project fail.

The building program of 1883 was an especially big one. Van Horne set an objective of three miles of new track per day for the prairie area. The objective was not always reached, but on some occasions it was far exceeded. Nine miles of track in a single day was considered a construction record.

On August 11, 1883, almost exactly eight years after Inspector Brisebois led his troop of Mounted Police into the Bow Valley to choose a site for a fort, the rails were laid to the east side of the Elbow River, where Calgary stands today. Some of those who watched had never seen a train. Before the end of that season, rails were laid to the summit of Kicking Horse Pass, near Lake Louise. The route ahead was by Kicking Horse River Valley, Donald, Rogers Pass in the Selkirk Range, and Revelstoke. Clearly, the most difficult railroad construction was yet to be undertaken, where mountains had to be tunnelled, gorges to be bridged, and the necessary precautions taken against snow and rock slides.

Actually, however, construction was already proceeding from the West, as Ottawa leaders sought to appease local indignation caused by delay. British Columbia people did not allow the federal government to forget its promises about railroad construction. Was not a railroad to be started within two years after the British Columbia entry into the Union and finished within 10 years? Construction did begin on a Vancouver Island line on July 19, 1873, just one day before the first period of two years would elapse. Nevertheless, there was not enough activity to convince coastal residents of government intentions. After John A. Macdonald's defeat, his successor in office was unable to make a compromise arrangement with the British Columbia government and Premier Walkem appealed to Queen Victoria. The British government appointed Lord Carnarvon to look into the situation and received his report recommending that work be directed at building the Esquimalt-Nanaimo railroad on the island, completion of the survey on the mainland, a telegraph line and wagon road through the mountains, and completion of a railroad between the Great Lakes and the west coast by the end of 1890.

The British Columbia people might have accepted this, but there was no indication of a guarantee from Ottawa, and they became more and more annoyed. What Lord Dufferin, the Governor General, saw when he visited Victoria was an archway bearing the words: "Carnarvon Terms Or Separation." Walkem was returned to power in the province in 1878 on a policy of obtaining satisfaction from Ottawa or seeking secession. He went so far as to set a date in May 1879 for withdrawal from the Canadian union, if an acceptable arrangement were not made in the meantime.

As it turned out, Sir John A. Macdonald was back in power by that date and the prospect of realizing the railroad brightened. Sir John gave fresh

The spiral tunnel at Mount Stephen in British Columbia.

assurances, and in the next year, 1880, workers began building the grade eastward from Port Moody, on Burrard Inlet. Andrew Onderdonk was the contractor, responsible for building along the Fraser and on as far as Savona. Much of it was terrifying and forbidding terrain.

Thousands of men were now employed, working from both East and West, blasting, digging, tunnelling, and finally, on November 7, 1885, the construction crews met at Craigellachie, deep in the mountains, and there Donald Smith, better known as Lord Strathcona, hammered in the last spike to complete the longest railroad in the world and provide a tangible tie between East and West.

A government promise, although a little late, was made good. The first train from Montreal drew into Port Moody on July 4, 1886, amid loud enthusiasm from local people. But something more was needed at the western terminus: a deep-sea harbour. Before long, the rails were being laid to that more suitable harbour, and there, the city of Vancouver arose.

Following completion of the C.P.R., the most courageous effort of them all, various other schemes for transcontinental railways were advanced, with two of them to be realized. The famous construction team, Mackenzie and Mann, built the Canadian Northern in bits and pieces, but not without a plan, and ultimately drove it to completion in 1915. It used the Yellowhead Pass route through the mountains, then to Kamloops, and along the Fraser River Canyon to Vancouver. The Grand Trunk, also using the Sandford Fleming or Yellowhead Pass route, was built to reach the Pacific at Prince Rupert and offer the shortest rail distance across the continent. It was completed in 1914.

Other railways were built on more modest scales. In Alberta there was the Northern Alberta Railway and in British Columbia, the Pacific Great Eastern, which was taken over by the provincial government in 1918.

But railroads, in some instances, were overbuilt, inviting financial difficulties. The Canadian Northern became bankrupt and was taken over in 1918 by the Government of Canada. The same fate befell the Grand Trunk, and by 1923, the federal government, more from necessity than choice, was welding several bankrupt lines and several other government-owned lines into the Canadian National Railway system.

One way or another, Canada emerged with the third largest network of railroads in the world. Some observers believed the country had more miles of railroads than it needed and certain lines could be abandoned. However that might be, railroads did serve the nation very well.

The Rush of Settlers

After purchasing the West, the Government of Canada acted promptly to put the newly-acquired property to use. One of the first needs was for a land survey. A start had been made in 1869, but it was suspended rudely by Louis Riel and his followers. In returning to the job after the trouble, however, workers were able to profit from earlier mistakes.

When William McDougall, as Minister of Public Works in the John A. Macdonald government, directed Col. J. S. Dennis to proceed with a survey prior to the insurrection, the land unit was to be a township consisting of 64 sections. That township would be nine miles by nine miles in size, and each section would contain 800 acres.

The Métis were opposed to any survey differing from the riverlot plan with which they were familiar. They made their dislike for the new plan very obvious, and in the recess created by the insurrection, government officials concluded that an 800-acre section was too big anyway. When the work was resumed in 1871, the survey was along the lines of the now familiar pattern in which the township unit consists of 36 sections, each of the latter containing 640 acres.

Surveyors required base lines. The international boundary, the 49th parallel, offered an east-west line while north-south lines called meridians were marked to provide bases at right angles to the boundary. Township rows would be numbered from the international boundary northward, and range rows would be numbered from meridian lines. Thus a land description like N.W.23–31–18–W2 would identify the northwest quarter of Section 23, in the 31st row of townships north from the boundary, and in the 18th perpendicular row of townships west of the second meridian. With such a description, it was possible to locate a piece of land on the map or in the field.

The government instructed that the survey was to proceed with all possible dispatch. The Dominion Lands Act was formally passed on April 14, 1872, and later in that year, 40 survey parties were in the field. But the survey was not a job to be completed in a season or two. The peak of field operations was not reached until 1883, and even then there were problems in staying ahead of the growing flood of incoming settlers.

The new land regulations invited homestead applications from adults prepared to pay fees of $10 per quarter section and willing to meet five-year residence requirements in order to qualify for titles. Nevertheless, there was no immediate rush for homesteads. Most prospective settlers wanted more assurance that a quarter-section farm in some remote part of the continent was worth the time and trouble. They also wanted the benefit of a railroad.

A few groups were still willing to brave the uncertainties of a frontier. The Mennonites, looking for religious freedom, came from Russia and were the first of the immigrants from Europe to arrive in numbers. Their choice of location had a special significance. Having engaged in farming on the Russian plains, they had no fear of the treeless country and went boldly to the prairies south of Winnipeg. There they established themselves in colonies. Many of the young Mennonites obtained good educations and became Manitoba leaders.

Then came the Icelandic people who settled mainly on the west side of Lake Winnipeg where they could combine farming and fishing. The earliest groups tried Wisconsin and eastern Canada, but in 1875, most of the Icelanders were moving on to Manitoba where they founded the town of Gimli and an enterprising community. An epidemic of smallpox added to the hardships of the first winter in Manitoba, but the people persevered and gained the reputation of being thrifty and resourceful. In the years that followed, many of them became leaders in business, the professions, and politics.

It was perfectly clear that somebody would have to pay for the construction of the railroad. The small population, only 66,000 in Manitoba and not many more in the entire Northwest in 1881, could not be expected to do it. The obvious need, as both the Government of Canada and the C.P.R. saw it, was for settlers, and it was hoped that the attraction of free land coupled with the conveniences of the new railroad would bring them.

After granting 25 million acres to the C.P.R. in 1881, homestead regulations had to be changed. The railway company was to receive all odd-numbered sections in townships lying up to 24 miles on both sides of the railway, and the change of policy in 1882 restricted homesteads to even-numbered sections, exclusive of school land and sections 8 and three-quarters of 26 which were reserved for the Hudson's Bay Company. The same entry fee of $10 was charged, but residence requirements were reduced to three years.

As the flow of landseekers increased, the gateway city of Winnipeg boomed. Its population reached 10,000 in 1881, and local people obtained their earliest vision of a great metropolis. Many of the newcomers halted at Winnipeg to buy equipment, horses, oxen, wagons, flour, and anything else likely to be needed. The Winnipeg merchants were delighted.

John Sanderson was the first man to homestead in the West. He set up his home five miles from Portage la Prairie on July 2, 1872.

Canada Department of Immigration and Colonization

Both the government and railway companies became increasingly anxious for land settlement and various schemes were tried. What was known as halfbreed scrip, intended originally to settle a debt with the Métis people, was given out fairly freely. A scrip was good for any crown quarter open for either sale or settlement, but it was transferable, and many of the certificates were exchanged for guns or whisky.

For a while, colonization companies seemed the most promising instruments in gaining rapid land occupation. From 1882 onward, a properly constituted company could obtain a tract of land beyond 24 miles from the C.P.R. main line and branch lines, or beyond 12 miles of any other projected railroad. The even-numbered sections were reserved for homesteads and pre-emptions, but the company could buy the odd-numbered ones at $2.00 per acre while undertaking to place settlers at the rate of two per section within five years. Having fulfilled their part, the company men might qualify for a rebate on the original purchase price from the government. Colonization companies flourished for a time, and at the end of 1883, at least 26 companies holding 2,973,978 acres of land were actively engaged in settlement.

In many cases, immigrants remained in ethnic communities where they could enjoy the company of their own people. The Cannington Manor Colony, south of Moosomin, was the dream of Captain Pierce who thought of it as a settlement in which Englishmen coming to the frontier might remain close to their own folks, living as Englishmen like to live, with time for cricket, fox-hunting, and tea at 4 o'clock. The Pierce family arrived to take up residence in January 1883 and drove the 45 miles from Moosomin when winter weather was at its worst. The Barr Colony at Lloydminster was started some years later, and it, too, was intensely English in character. Just as Cannington Manor attracted Englishmen and Gimli attracted Icelanders, the Temperance Colony in which the city of Saskatoon had its origin was for those, and those alone, who shunned strong drink.

With the rising tide of settlement, it seemed that all countries in Europe and some outside Europe were represented. Many Jews came to Canada in the eighties, some of them settling in the West. Hungarians came to Manitoba in 1882, and four years later, more were assisted by Count Paul d'Esterhazy in settling around the village now bearing his name in southeastern Saskatchewan. Germans found the West about 1890, many of them following Father Bruno and settling around Humboldt. Scandinavians became fairly numerous and proved excellent citizens. Settlers from the United States may have outnumbered any other nationality.

The Mormons, who arrived in 1887, accounted for part of the influx from the south. Charles Ora Card, son-in-law of Brigham Young, left Utah to search for a new location and arrived at Calgary late in 1886.

There he bought a team of horses, wagon, and plow with which to test the soil. After examining the High River area, he went to Lee's Creek where he found what he wanted. In the next summer, 12 families came by covered wagon and settled where the town of Cardston stands today.

Ukrainian settlers from southern Russia made their first appearance in the West in 1891 and came in larger numbers in 1898. They were the men in sheepskins, choosing parkland locations where they built thatched homes, outdoor ovens, and made various kinds of equipment to prove their resourcefulness.

Also from southern Russia came the Doukhobors, who were pacifists and vegetarians. Some of the earliest arrivals were assisted by Count Leo Tolstoy and took land around the village of Veregin. In 1899, seven thousand came to what is now northeastern Saskatchewan.

The most important date in the history of immigration and land settlement was 1896, when Clifford Sifton became Minister of the Interior and set about to attract more immigrants than ever before. The annual entry rose steadily to reach a peak of 400,870 immigrants in 1913. Not all the immigrants became homesteaders, but many did adopt the land. It must not be overlooked that even in the heaviest years of immigration, the United States was a big contributor of settlers. In the first decade of the present century, 44 per cent of the homestead entries made in western Canada were by immigrants from the United States.

In this way, the West was settled by people of many nationalities, each bringing their own cultural distinctiveness, each finding fresh loyalty for their land of adoption.

The Ranch Herds

Grass was one of the first natural resources to catch the white man's roving eye. It invited grazing, and as a result, trade in meats.

On the Alberta side of the mountains, ranching had to wait for a reduction in the number of buffalo and the Indians' acceptance of the principle of private ownership. On the British Columbia side, cattlemen waited only for markets. Consequently, ranch cattle occupied intermountain valleys for some years before Constable Whitney released the first herd to test a winter on the short-grass plains.

A meat-hungry gold rush population provided the first inducement for cattlemen who drove herds from the Oregon Territory for the express purpose of slaughter and sale as fresh beef. When the gold rush ended, the remaining cattle were turned loose to fend for themselves and demonstrate how well they could adjust to those intermountain ranges. Cattlemen watched with interest.

Lewis "Shifty" Campbell and "Gypsie" Johnny Wilson were not the first to drive cattle to the Interior for slaughter, but they may have been the first to introduce breeding stock. Wilson was the gypsy lad who left his nomadic people in England to make his way in the New World, and Lewis Campbell was the son of an Indiana farmer for whom Wilson worked after arriving on the continent. Both young fellows were present at the gold diggings in California and then in British Columbia. Although they were not travelling together, their ideas were about the same, and after driving herds for slaughter to the British Columbia gold fields, both thought about raising cattle right there.

By 1864, Campbell was settling down a few miles east of Kamloops, and there he and his friend of former years decided to pool their resources and bring in a breeding herd. Early in 1865, the two men were riding southward, Wilson carrying the bag of gold dust with which to pay for cattle purchased, and Campbell carrying the loaded guns for the protection of the gold. They bought 300 head of breeding stock and turned the herd toward British Columbia. There were broad rivers like the Columbia to be crossed by swimming, and dangerous passes to be overcome by hard driving. There were hostile Indians along the way and hazards in many other forms but, ultimately, men and cattle reached the Wilson and Campbell range near Kamloops. The two men later dissolved the partnership, but both continued to breed cattle and became big operators on the British Columbia grass.

The Harper Brothers, Jerome and Thaddeus, as noted previously, drove cattle from Oregon Territory to the Fraser River mining camps in each of three years: 1862, 1863, and 1864. When the last herd could not be sold for beef, the Harpers decided to try ranching on those good intermountain ranges. Jerome Harper died a few years later, but Thaddeus carried on, and it was he who directed the big herd overland to San Francisco in 1876.

But the distinction of being the most influential cattleman in the early years must go to Joseph Greaves of Douglas Lake Ranch, in British Columbia's Nicola Valley. As a boy he ran away from his Yorkshire, England, home and came to North America as a stowaway on the sailing ship, *Patrick Henry*. When he was discovered on board, his punishment came from the ship's captain who ordered him to feed and look after the pigs carried on the voyage. At New York, the boy obtained work with a local farmer, but very soon thereafter he joined a wagon train about to cross the continent to the California gold diggings.

After California, public interest shifted to the Fraser River and Greaves announced that he was going, but he had a hunch that he might make more profit by selling meat than by digging in the gravel. He drove a flock of sheep from the Dalles to Olympia on the coast and there found it possible

Alberta Publicity and Travel Bureau

A ranching scene in the foothills.

to ship them to the mouth of the Fraser. Then, after the long drive into the Interior, Greaves slaughtered the sheep and sold the mutton at prices which induced him to return to Oregon for more animals for slaughter. On the second and third trips he drove cattle, but the demand was falling, and the last herd was turned loose at Walachin, beside the Thompson River.

Now and again Greaves would conduct a roundup and cut out a few fat cattle to be driven to New Westminster. The herd was growing faster than local demand, however, and there are stories about 4,000 of Greaves' cattle being driven in the direction of Chicago in 1880. As told by one who later worked with Greaves, the drive ended at a point in southeastern Wyoming where there was the advantage of a railway connection with Chicago.

Greaves was said to return to British Columbia with fresh determination to expand his cattle-raising operations. By this time, the C.P.R. was projected westward, and any man with vision could see markets developing. In 1882, Greaves entered into a partnership with friends to conduct ranching on a much bigger scale at Douglas Lake. He bought hundreds of breeding cattle, and in a short time, his ranch was the biggest beef-producing enterprise in Canada, and its ultimate record made it the oldest.

On the prairie side of the Rockies, interest in cattle-ranching followed quickly upon the disappearance of the buffalo herds. Kootenai Brown had noted that where buffalo flourished, cattle should be able to do the same. He was right. The buffalo was a good judge of grass and had shown a preference for the short but highly nutritious grass of the plains.

In 1878, just a year after Constable Robert Whitney's cattle passed the important survival test outdoors in winter, George Emerson and Tom Lynch drove a thousand cattle from Montana and allowed them to roam on the good grass beside the Highwood River. With no fences in the country, the cattle could wander far in any direction, and the Emerson and Lynch animals became fat and sleek.

The Hon. M. H. Cochrane, from Compton, Quebec, was the next to make cattle history in foothills' country. Driving a democrat and team of ponies, he appeared in that part early in 1881, in order to make his own assessment of ranching opportunities. He met up with Kootenai Brown who told him that the future for cattle was as favourable as in Montana. Cochrane was convinced and rushed away to secure a federal government grazing lease on 100,000 acres west of Calgary. Later in the year, a herd of 3,000 Montana cattle, most of them showing their close relationship to Texas Longhorns, appeared on the trail leading to the Bow River. Men of the I. G. Baker Company, commissioned to deliver the herd, were trying to reach the new ranch headquarters at Big Hill, beside today's town of Cochrane, before winter weather overtook them. Major James Walker, who had retired from the Mounted Police to become Cochrane's ranch manager, received the herd under most adverse circumstances. The cattle were thin and tired, and the winter weather which followed was severe. Winter losses were heavy, but Cochrane was determined to succeed with his experiment, and a second herd was being driven over the trail toward Calgary in the autumn of 1882. This one reached the foothills in time to feel the icy sting of an early snowstorm. Once again the Cochrane losses were heavy enough to discourage or ruin any ordinary person.

Believing that a more southerly range would be less risky, Cochrane obtained a lease between the Oldman and Waterton Rivers and moved all his cattle to it. In spite of the transfer, ill fortune continued to follow the pioneer herd, and in the very first winter after the change, the range west of Calgary enjoyed freedom from heavy snows while the southern range was blanketed with drifts. But Cochrane, the first of the prairie Cattle Barons, persisted and better luck attended later ranch efforts.

The next big herd to be driven over the trails to what is now Alberta was that of the North West Cattle Company, owned by the Allans of Montreal. It was the beginning of the famous Bar U Ranch with which the name of George Lane, one of Alberta's "Big Four" ranchers, was long associated.

In delivering the original herd late in 1882, Tom Lynch, "king of the cattle trails", introduced some particularly able American cowboys and cattle-men to Canadian soil, among them the great Negro rancher, John Ware.

After 1882, the big herds were more numerous. The Oxley herd, with English capital and monocled directors, started in that year, while the Walrond outfit appeared in 1883 and the Quorn in 1884. In fact, by 1884, 2,782,000 acres of grazing land were held in 41 leases, mainly in the well favoured foothills. The Cochrane Ranch had the biggest herd east of the mountains at that time, with the I. G. Baker Company, the North West Cattle Company, and Walrond Ranch ranking second, third, and fourth in size.

Ranching continued to prosper for several years and then received its near-ruinous setback. It was the winter of 1886-87. The preceding summer was hot and dry, and with a rapid expansion in the herds, some ranges were overgrazed and bare. An early winter, heavy snows, low temperatures, and an absence of chinooks combined to make it the worst winter cattlemen had experienced. Cattle drifted in the storms, and many perished in the coulees. A rancher who was present estimated that 40 per cent of all cattle south of the Red Deer River died during that fateful winter. When the snow melted in the spring, the countryside was littered with rotting car-casses, and many ranchers faced bankruptcy. Nevertheless, the bad winter served to furnish lessons about ranch management, and the cattle industry was rehabilitated with more thought being directed to reserves of feed and the animals' winter needs.

The Cochrane Ranch, the outfit which brought the first big cattle herd to the foothills and prairies, also brought the first flock of ranch sheep. Although never popular with the cattlemen, sheep deserved their chance on the Canadian range, and the Cochrane management wanted something to eat the grass on the range west of Calgary after cattle were moved to a more southerly location. Accordingly, late in 1884, a flock consisting of 8,000 sheep was being driven from Montana to Big Hill, by way of Calgary. Cattlemen continued their campaign against sheep in the best grass coun-try, arguing that grazing sheep left the range unsatisfactory for cattle. The Cochrane sheep did meet with moderate success, however, and other big flocks followed into what is now southern Alberta and southwestern Saskatchewan.

Incoming settlers encroached upon country the cattlemen would have chosen to keep for their exclusive use, and the Canadian ranchland had to be limited to areas considered unsuitable for cropping. Inevitably, ranching changed greatly from the years of open range and country-wide roundups, but in much of the British Columbia interior, the Alberta foothills, and on the most arid part of the prairies, the ranch cattle industry continued to be important. In those areas where it survives as a specialized branch of agriculture, ranching represents the best possible use of land.

The Pioneer Newspapers

In those years prior to radio and television, the newspaper was the settlers' only source of information. It was important for newcomers to the country to know where equipment could be bought and at what prices. It was useful for every one to know what was happening in other parts, and it was reassuring to have an editor who had the courage to speak and write boldly against injustices. Settlers would have agreed with H. L. Mencken, who considered that one of the roles of the press was to comfort the afflicted and afflict the comfortable. It was a role into which men like Amor de Cosmos, John Robson, Patrick Gammie Laurie, Frank Oliver, and Nicholas Flood Davin fitted perfectly.

Any aspiring editor with the courage to start a newspaper could be assured of a frontier welcome, but preparations for printing were never easy. The earliest western papers were printed on presses brought to the country well in advance of a railroad. This necessitated transporting heavy equipment by cart or canoe and often over great distances.

Victoria, British Columbia, led the way for the entire West, while Winnipeg had the first printing press between the Great Lakes and the mountains. The *British Colonist*, a small sheet making its first appearance on December 11, 1858, was the brainchild of Amor de Cosmos, who came to Victoria with the first wave of miners making their way to the Fraser River gold fields. Editor de Cosmos fancied a challenge, and no voice rang more clearly than his in support of the union of Vancouver Island and the mainland colony of British Columbia and, later, the entry of British Columbia into Confederation. Although the name was changed slightly, the *Colonist* was still a journalistic force more than a hundred years after its birth and almost synonymous with the name of the city in which it was published.

On the prairies, the *Nor'-Wester*, published by partners William Buckingham and William Caldwell, was the undisputed pioneer newspaper. Printed on a press carted from St. Paul, Minnesota, to Fort Garry by the two young Englishmen, its fortunes were mixed indeed. A subscription price of five dollars a year was enough to keep most Red River citizens off the customer list, but all who were able to read, a small percentage of the total population, were anxious to see every issue. The paper appeared on December 28, 1859, and made an impression from the beginning, especially upon the Hudson's Bay Company, whose monopolistic trading practices were the principal objects of editorial attack.

When the *Nor'-Wester* was taken over by Dr. John Schultz, later Lieutenant Governor of Manitoba, the attacks were even more bitter. But the

Schultz criticism of the Louis Riel campaign brought him trouble. After Riel set up his provisional government in 1869, he seized the *Nor'-Wester* and used the equipment to print his own paper, the *New Nation*, and then to print his manifesto to the citizens of Red River. And for the editor himself, Riel had a nice prison cell in Fort Garry.

The midwestern paper with the longest unbroken record was Winnipeg's *Free Press*, first published as the *Weekly Free Press* in 1872. The *Winnipeg Tribune*, also with a long record of publication, was started in 1889.

The *Saskatchewan Herald*, published at Battleford by tall, Scottish Patrick Gammie Laurie, was distinctive in many ways. Laurie had worked with the *Nor'-Wester* and then the *Weekly Free Press* and knew a considerable amount about frontier problems. His aim, however, was to work for himself. To this end, he had the primitive printing press with which he produced his paper hauled by Red River cart over the long trail from St. Paul to Winnipeg and then the longer trail from Winnipeg to Battleford on the North Saskatchewan River. The initial issue, dated August 25, 1878, gave Laurie the distinction of being the first publisher between Winnipeg and the Rockies.

Laurie, who saw the Cree Indians attack Battleford during the rebellion days of 1885, left some of the best accounts of events at that historic period. He acknowledged the Métis grievances as legitimate, but took a strong stand against the ruthless methods employed by the insurgents.

The next newspaper adventure was made by Frank Oliver, who saw Fort Edmonton as a freighter on the long trail, and then hauled his printing press the thousand miles from Winnipeg to launch the *Edmonton Bulletin* in 1880. Indeed, he hauled this piece of heavy equipment over the trail not once but twice. On the first trip, he was just more than half way to his destination when the raft being used to ferry the precious press across the North Saskatchewan River capsized, and the press sank to the bottom of the river where it was to remain forever.

Oliver, who became a leading public figure, was not one to accept defeat, and he simply returned to Winnipeg where he obtained another press. On the second trip, the press was delivered successfully, and in the first issue of the *Bulletin*, appearing on December 6, 1880, the editor reported such news as John Coutts' arrival "with ten carts loaded with bacon from Carlton", and the awarding of a mail contract for the Winnipeg-Edmonton section of the country to Sinclair and McLane.

The *Macleod Gazette*, started in 1882, and the *Calgary Herald*, beginning in 1883, deserve special mention. The difficulties encountered by the man behind the *Gazette* were not entirely unusual. C. E. D. Wood, ex-mounted policeman, placed an order in Toronto for a printing press a full year before the paper appeared. The machine was shipped by Duluth and

THE BULLETIN.

| Vol. I. | EDMONTON, N.W.T., DECEMBER 6, 1880. | Number 1. |

NO TELEGRAMS.

As the line has been down since Saturday between Hay Lakes and here, we are without telegrams for this issue. A man will leave to-morrow to repair it, and by next week we hope to be able to give the latest news from the East up to date.

"HEWALD" EXTRA.

The following extra from the "Saskatchewan Herald" office arrived here by last mail:—

BATTLEFORD, Nov. 22, 1880.

By Cable to the "Herald.—LONDON, Nov. 15.— Hanlan beat Trickett by three boat lengths, winning the championship of the world.

From Winnipeg.—Garfield, Republican, has been elected President of the United States.

A provisional contract has been signed by which the syndicate binds itself to complete the prairie Section of the C.P.R. in three years

It is said there is great trouble among the people (original copy too indistinct) have been shot, and should there not be a change in the aspect of affairs a revolution is imminent

REDUCING THE FORCE.—Eastern papers say that the Department of the Interior, having concluded to reduce the number of officers in charge of the Mounted Police by six, the position made vacant by the death of the late Superintendent Dalrymple Clarke will not be filled. There are to be no immediate dismissals, but as officers are removed by the hand of death, or voluntarily send in their resignations, their respective offices will be abolished, and the work divided up among those remaining.

The Government has relieved Mr. Ryan of the contract for the first hundred miles of the C.P.R. west of Winnipeg, and will proceed with the construction in a more substantial manner than his contract called for—and, it is to be hoped, a little quicker.

The Scott Temperance Act has been carried by a large majority in Marquette County, Manitoba. The people of Portage la Prairie have entered a protest against it. They don't know what is good for themselves.

Track was laid on the C.P.R. east of Winnipeg to within three miles of Rat Portage at last accounts. The weekly mail service has been extended to Bird Tail Creek settlement.

Sitting Bull is again talking of going south.

LOCAL.

MR. A. LANG has captured a young silver grey fox around Edmonton.

A SPECIAL CONSTABLE is to be sworn in for duty around Edmonton.

REV. MR. STEINHAUER, of White Fish Lake, lately addressed the Methodist conference in Montreal.

MR. CUST has the contract for the Indian Department flour at $7.50 for Edmonton delivery and $8.50 for Victoria.

GEORGE GLGNON lately killed a very large wolf which, after disposing of one of his sheep, came back for another.

THE sheep lately imported from Montana by J. Volier, and sold in this district are doing much better than was expected.

ALEX. McDONALD and Albert Boyd left for Bow River to-day. The former expects to return to Edmonton next April to start farming.

MR. GLASS has started a subscription list for the purpose of supplying the Methodist Mission church with firewood, oil, etc., for the winter.

ABRAM SPLEYN and others from the Battle River settlement 50 miles from here, brought the first grist to the Edmonton Mills to-day—31 bushels of barley.

NEW YEAR'S DAY is drawing nigh, and we have not heard of a thing being done about the grand show. Would it not be advisable to start the ball.

A BIG LAKE resident wants to know why the Government potatoe contract was not awarded to him, seeing that his offer was 20 cents lower than that of the party who secured it.

MR. LUCAS, Government farmer at Peace Hills, has been supplied with his share of that band of cows. They are reported to be the sickest looking lot of animals in the country.

THE following are the ruling prices for produce in this vicinity:—Oats $1.00 per bushel of 34 lbs., wheat $2.00 to $2.50, barley $1.00, pease .25 per lb., potatoes $1.00, onions $2.00, and butter .50.

LAST Saturday morning the thermometers at Fts. Edmonton and Saskatchewan registered 47 below zero. This cold snap, which set in last Tuesday, is much more severe than the corresponding one last year, but appears to be about over.

MR. WM. CUST is in a bad fix about his threshing. Lamoreaux threshed out 1,000 bushels on his Sturgeon River farm, and quit, leaving two stacks unthreshed, and says that he will set fire to his machine rather than thresh another bushel, while Smith is going to quit threshing, on account of the cold and make shingles for the rest of the winter.

The first issue of "The Bulletin", published in December 1880.

Stanley A. Williams

Bismark, to be forwarded by riverboat to Fort Benton, Montana. Riverboats were unpredictable, however, and with the low water level in the Missouri, part of the boat's freight, including the press, had to be unloaded and left on the riverbank. There, with no protection except that afforded by a tarpaulin, the press remained until high water in the spring, when a Benton-bound boat stopped and picked it up. Finally, Wood's press was delivered at Fort Macleod by ox-drawn freight wagons, bull trains, from Fort Benton. The first issue of the *Gazette* came off on July 1, 1882, telling about eight pure-bred bulls being brought in for Captain Stewart's ranch and 800 beef steers arriving to furnish beef rations for the Blood and Piegan Indians.

The pioneer editors, many more than mentioned, made notable records from a point of view of service. Some went into politics and became national figures, some remained in journalism, and a few served time in jail. In nearly all instances, the editors were progressive individuals whose influence and guidance in developing communities were valuable indeed.

Battle Lines on the South Saskatchewan

What was known as halfbreed scrip, distributed after the Red River trouble in 1869-70, did not reach to the root of the Métis problem. Instead of exchanging the certificates for Crown land, most of the native people traded them off recklessly and continued to fret about the sweep of settlers crowding in upon them. Many of the Red River Métis moved farther west to locations like those on the South Saskatchewan River, hoping to continue the wild, free lives they loved and be away from the incoming white man.

Once again, however, civilization was overtaking them, resulting in destruction of the buffalo herds and an end to freedom as they knew it. Naturally, they were irritated, and when they petitioned the Government of Canada for aid, nothing of consequence happened. What the aggrieved people wanted was security, perhaps a Métis province where they could administer in their own way.

The fears felt by those along the South Saskatchewan, north of Saskatoon, were expressed clearly in a letter to Sir John A. Macdonald dated September 4, 1882, and signed by the great native leader, Gabriel Dumont, and 46 others:

> Sir—We the undersigned French half-breeds, for the most part settled on the west bank of the Saskatchewan, in the district of Prince Albert, N.W.T., hereby approach you, in order to set forth with confidence the painful position in which we are placed with reference to the lands occupied by us in this portion of the territory, and in order to call the attention of the Government to the questions which cause us so much anxiety. Compelled, most of us, to abandon the prairie, which can no longer furnish us the means of subsistence, we came in large numbers, during the course of the summer and settled on the south branch of the Saskatchewan. Pleased with the land and the country, we set ourselves actively to work clearing the land. . . . The surveyed lands being already occupied or sold, we were compelled to occupy lands not yet surveyed, being ignorant, for the most part, also, of the regulations of the Government respecting Dominion lands. Great then was our astonishment and perplexity when we were notified that when the lands were surveyed we shall be obliged to pay $2 an acre to the Government if our lands are included in odd-numbered sections. We desire, moreover, to keep close together, in order more easily to secure a school and a church. We are poor people and cannot pay for our land without utter ruin. . . . In our anxiety we appeal to your sense of justice as Minister of the Interior and head of the Government, and beg you to reassure us speedily by directing that we shall not be disturbed on our lands, and that the Government grant us the privilege of considering us as occupants of even-numbered sections, since we have occupied these lands in good faith. Having so long held this country as its masters . . . we consider it not asking too much to request that the Government allow us to occupy our lands in peace. . . . We also pray that you would direct that the lots be surveyed along the river ten chains in width by two miles in depth, this mode of division being the long established usage of the country. This would render it more easy for us to know the limits of our several lots. We trust, Sir, that you will grant a favourable hearing to this our petition.
>
> *Sessional Paper, No. 45, Vol. 12,* 1886.

Lack of response to the letter gave reason to believe that the officials had forgotten the Red River experience of 1869. Gabriel Dumont tried again, writing on February 1, 1883, to the Lieutenant Governor of Territories. The request was for land grants, help in building a school, aid in buying farm equipment and seed grain, and finally, that members of the halfbreed community be considered for the next appointments to the Council of the North West Territories.

Had the Métis position been examined sympathetically, the violence of 1885 might have been avoided. The Mounted Police and members of the Territorial Council were well aware of the dangers. As it was, the apparent indifference to their plight angered Dumont's people. They wanted action. They knew Dumont as a great hunter and great fighter, but they still thought of Louis Riel as the matchless leader. They wanted Riel, and late in 1884, a deputation travelled by horse to Montana where Riel was teaching school. He agreed to come, and very soon, residents along the river were rallying to him as they had done 15 years earlier.

Riel's personality had changed and he was, by this time, fanatically religious. Dumont, on the other hand, was ready for violence. Major Crozier, with police and volunteers from Prince Albert, responded to a call from settlers who saw their suppliers being plundered and, on March 26, came face to face with Dumont and a following of heavily armed men. A shot was fired and a battle followed. After 12 men were killed and 25 wounded, the Prince Albert troop withdrew, conceding clear victory to the Métis.

A committee was now named to investigate the Métis claims, but it was too late. Nothing could be more certain than further fighting. The greatest danger was in the Indians on reservations being persuaded to take to the warpath. There can be no doubt that Riel and Dumont sent runners to encourage an Indian uprising. Young Indians favoured the idea of rebellion and massacre on a broad scale, but most of the older ones like Crowfoot and Piapot succeeded in restraining their people. Big Bear was not as successful in holding back his Plains Crees, and he saw them attack the mission at Frog Lake, killing nine men, including two priests, government agent Thomas Quinn, and several settlers. At the same time, Chief Poundmaker's Crees went against Battleford, where 500 frightened citizens sought refuge in the Mounted Police barracks and hoped for the best. The Poundmaker Indians looted Battleford homes and set fire to some.

Fort Pitt, a Mounted Police post under the command of Inspector Francis Dickens, son of the English novelist, seemed to be in for the same kind of massacre as that directed at Frog Lake, but the police, acting upon advice from the Hudson's Bay Factor, William MacLean, abandoned the fort and went down river by scow. Wisely, too, the Company man at Fort

Pitt turned his wife and children to Big Bear's mercy, and they were unharmed.

News of conflict reached the East, with headlines telling: "Riel Leading New War Against Whites", all that was needed to shock the Ontario citizens who had not forgotten or forgiven the man responsible for the shooting of Thomas Scott. Quickly, a military force under command of General Middleton made ready for service in the West. Toronto citizens felt that the rebellious groups had to be put down at any price.

For Middleton's army, travel to the scene of hostilities was certain to present serious difficulties because the C.P.R. was not completed. Nevertheless, Van Horne, as manager, told Sir John A. Macdonald he would deliver troops to western points on the railway in 11 days. Knowing that certain portions of the road were still incomplete, necessitating travel by sleigh, Sir John believed it could not be done. But Van Horne made good his promise, and in less than a month, 3,000 men were on the prairies, ready for battle.

The new railroad, even though unfinished, proved its essential value to the country, and the national emergency, in turn, did as much for the railroad by bringing needed help at a time when the syndicate was facing financial crisis.

Colonel Otter's brigade approaching the South Saskatchewan River in 1885.

Mrs. J. R. Metcalfe

The plan of attack called for three columns to advance northward from the C.P.R. Middleton and his portion of the army left Qu'Appelle and travelled toward Batoche with the idea of engaging the main body of the insurgents. Col. Otter and his force went northward from Swift Current for the purpose of relieving the Battleford settlement and dealing a blow to Poundmaker's Indians. The third field force, under General Strange, a retired British Army officer who had taken to ranching on the Bow River, went north from Calgary to Edmonton, where the settlers were plainly nervous.

Middleton's men engaged the Métis at Fish Creek and did not fare very well. Otter's force travelled westward from Battleford to engage Poundmaker's Indians at Cut Knife Hill. For Otter, the adventure proved humiliating. There was a race to gain the presumed advantage of the hill, but there is reason to believe the Indians actually hoped the whites would occupy it. The Crees then took the valley locations and surrounded the hill. Eight of Otter's men were killed and 14 wounded, and if the Cree chief had not restrained his warriors, the slaughter might have been as terrible as it was in General George Custer's last stand nine years earlier. As it was, Poundmaker mercifully allowed the white soldiers to escape.

In the important encounter at Batoche, on May 9, Middleton's force, with superior strength, succeeded in driving the Métis from their rifle pits and routing them. Riel escaped, but after a few days he gave himself up, tired, hungry, and disillusioned. Later, he was taken to Regina where he was tried, convicted, sentenced to be hanged and, rightly or wrongly, executed on November 16, 1885.

Most of the Métis laid down their arms. Dumont fled to the United States but did not stay there. Poundmaker and Big Bear surrendered and were tried on the charge of treason-felony and sentenced to prison. Both, however, were released before their terms had expired.

Riel's body, after the hanging, was taken for burial to St. Boniface, some people still regarding him as a murderer, some as a great hero. Eighty years later, controversy was still evident, but more and more people were regarding him as one who, having seen his fellow Métis suffering as a result of injustices, would have been less than a man if he had not drawn upon all the resources at his command in order to help them.

The shooting of Scott was, no doubt, a serious mistake, but in other respects, Riel's action was only that of a conscientious person fighting for common justice on behalf of his friends.

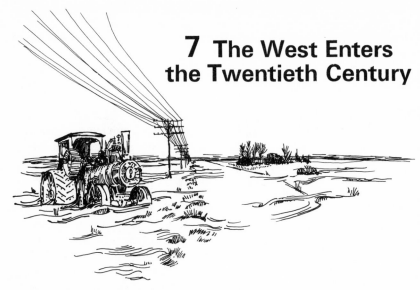

7 The West Enters the Twentieth Century

Into the Twentieth Century

The Canadian West entered the twentieth century like a growing boy, still a trifle awkward, but gaining confidence and ready to make his own way in the world.

As the new century dawned, the Hon. C. A. Semlin was the Premier of British Columbia and the Hon. Thomas Greenway was about to end his years as Premier of Manitoba. In the Territories, not considered ready for provincial government, the Hon. Frederick Haultain was the rather perpetual premier. At Ottawa, Prime Minister Sir Wilfrid Laurier was reminding all around him that the twentieth century belonged to Canada.

The population of the entire West, now Manitoba, Saskatchewan, Alberta, and British Columbia, was only a little more than half a million. The 1901 census showed it to be 598,169 with approximately 43 per cent of the total in Manitoba, 27 per cent in the North West Territories and 30 per cent in British Columbia. The all-western count was roughly 12½ per cent of what it would be 60 years later and considerably less than the number of people in Metropolitan Vancouver alone in 1961.

The majority of western people were homesteaders, accepting inconvenience and austerity for the chance of ultimate success as farmers. Homesteading meant living far back from settlements and working hard. A few steam engines had been introduced to the prairies for threshing, and a few water-wheels were in operation on British Columbia streams, but otherwise, the advantages of a machine age were still years away. In the lumber woods and on farms, the horse was unchallenged as a source of power. Just about every adult Westerner was a horseman, and every young Westerner aspired to be a horseman. A boy was scarcely ready for long pants until he could talk intelligently about martingales, swamp fever, and bone spavins.

Most Westerners of that period were young or relatively so. As might be expected in a population of young people, the death rate was low, so low that in many communities no steps had been taken to provide cemeteries. The circumstances invited exaggeration. One story to illustrate the high state of health and low incident of dying told of a young man living near Regina who wrote to aging parents in Nova Scotia, urging them to move to his beloved frontier town where nobody had been known to die. After much persuasion, the parents sold their home on the seaboard and moved to the West, but after being greeted by their son, the first awful spectacle to catch their attention was a funeral procession on the main street. "What's this?" the father asked with shocked amazement. Cheerfully, the son replied: "Don't let that worry you, Father. It's just our town undertaker who died this week from starvation."

Significantly enough, the West was soon to be acknowledged as an area where human health was really above average and life expectancy the best in Canada. In addition, men outnumbered women two to one in most districts. Consequently, most men were bachelors and most homestead cabins were more or less in disorder. In appealing for immigrants, officials did not fail to point out the exceptional opportunities for young women interested in matrimony and homemaking. "You'll be engaged in two

The thatched-roof home of a settler near Verigin, Saskatchewan, built about 1910.

Photo MacEwan

months and cooking in your own kitchen in four months after arriving," one promoter promised girls in an audience in England.

The flow of immigrant stock was increasing steadily under the Hon. Clifford Sifton's policies. He fancied "a stalwart peasant in a sheep-skin coat, born on the soil, whose forefathers have been farmers for ten generations, with a stout wife and half a dozen children". They were coming in ever larger numbers. As well as the thousands coming from overseas and from the south, many disillusioned miners were returning from the Klondike, satisfied to accept the more tranquil life of farming.

As far as national origin was concerned, the western Canadian population of that period was taking on the most varied hue on earth. Literally scores of countries were represented, and most newcomers could speak only their mother tongue. Many chose to remain in groups with their own people where they could keep their native languages and customs; others seemed just as ready to adopt Canadian ways as quickly as possible. In any case, a cross-section of the population illustrated it was a peculiar *mélange*.

Those circumstances should have fostered understanding and tolerance, and there is reason to believe they did. Certainly, the frontier of those years provided some of the best stories about brotherhood, such as were needed in many parts of the world a generation or two later. There was the John Ware story, for example. John Ware was the Negro who came out of slavery and was denied the opportunity to learn to read and write. Coming into Canada with the first North West Cattle Company herd in 1882, he was persuaded to remain. Notwithstanding handicaps, John Ware became a successful rancher. Even more significant, he became one of the most highly respected and most dearly loved of pioneers in his generation. When John Ware brought his bride from Calgary to his ranch cabin beside Sheep Creek on a winter day, awaiting to receive the newlyweds and offer a genuine frontier welcome were neighbour friends, some Irish, some American, some Mexican, some Métis. It was the spirit of the West at that time.

Western people were too busy to pause for a formal twentieth century celebration in 1900, but there was much in changing scenes to mark the occasion. New villages with general stores and country elevators were springing up so rapidly that even the Post Office Department had trouble in identifying names. Trails were being replaced with graded roads; better homes were appearing; trees were being planted; educational facilities were being extended; and men were talking about automobiles which, if shown to be safe and satisfactory, might make driving horses and buggies obsolete. It was difficult to imagine, but Winnipeg saw its first auto, one brought in by Prof. Kenrick, in 1901, and Calgary had an auto in 1903, a Stanley Steamer, owned by Rancher William F. Cochrane.

It was all very impressive, but nothing was doing more to bring stability to the area than the emergence of the two economic giants: forest products in British Columbia and wheat in the country east of the Rockies. Affected by drought, the wheat crop of 1900 was not particularly good, only 18 million bushels from two million seeded acres, but acreage had been increasing annually, and in 1901, the West harvested 63 million bushels from two and one-half million acres, an average yield of 25 bushels per acre. After improving their homestead quarter sections, farmers sensed dependable markets for wheat and wanted more land.

Sir Wilfrid Laurier said the twentieth century belonged to Canada. Some Canadians living in Manitoba and beyond said it belonged to the West.

Two More Provinces — Saskatchewan and Alberta

The Government of Canada appeared to be in no hurry about converting the North West Territories to provinces. Manitoba became a province three years after Confederation, and British Columbia was admitted four years after. Both showed commendable progress, and it was particularly difficult for men like Frederick Haultain to understand why the intervening country had to wait until 1905.

In the initial plan, the North West Territories were to have an appointed council to advise the Lieutenant Governor and work with him, but nothing done by the first council made any impression upon the government at Ottawa. Meetings had been a waste of the members' time, but a new North West Territories Act came into effect in 1876, clarifying the responsibilities of an Advisory Council. Fresh hope attended the appointment of another council, members of which – James Macleod, Hugh Richardson, and Mathew Ryan – met with Lieutenant Governor David Laird at Livingstone, not far from Fort Pelly, in March 1877. For the historic meeting, the pioneer officials came by stagecoach, sleigh, and dogteam. They passed ordinances for the protection of the dwindling buffalo herds and the prevention of prairie fires. Before the next meeting of the council, the territorial capital was moved to Battleford.

By the terms of the North West Territories Act of 1875, any area of a thousand square miles found to contain at least a thousand resident adults could be set up as an electoral district with the right to name a representative to sit on the council. The first to qualify was the District of Lorne, Prince Albert district, and following the first election held in country now marked by the provinces of Saskatchewan and Alberta, Lawrence Clarke took his seat at the council meeting at Battleford in May 1881. But appointed members showed resentment toward the first elected members, and Lawrence Clarke, sitting as the only one of his kind, had reason to feel lonely. By 1882, however, when the council began meeting at Regina,

Glenbow Foundation   Glenbow Foundation

(*l.*) *The Hon. Frank Oliver, member of the second Legislative Assembly of the N.W.T. at Regina.* (*r.*) *Sir Frederick Haultain, prominent in Territorial and Saskatchewan politics in the pioneer years.*

the number of elected members had increased to six, and the sense of loneliness was fleeting.

Nevertheless, the power exercised by the council was still largely illusory. The Lieutenant Governor was, in effect, the ruling force. Those people who thought seriously about democracy and wanted self-government were annoyed; others did not care.

The federal election of 1887 saw N. F. Davis from Alberta, W. D. Perley from Assiniboia East, Nicholas Flood Davin from Assiniboia West, and D. W. McDougall from Saskatchewan being sent to represent the new West in the House of Commons. As a consequence, Ottawa heard more about territorial problems and the act governing the area was amended to allow for a Legislative Assembly of 22 members, each to be elected for a term of three years.

After a territorial election, the first Legislative Assembly was convened at Regina late in 1888. Among the elected members was 31-year-old Frederick Haultain from Fort Macleod, whose statesman-like leadership was to prove especially valuable in later years. His election came just four years after the *Macleod Gazette* of September 26, 1884, reported the arrival by coach of this young man "who intends opening an office and practicing law". As he fraternized with cowboys, policemen, and Indians in the ranching community, his qualities of leadership became evident, and his entry into public life proved to be a good thing for the entire West. Almost at once he was the chairman of a four-man Advisory Committee, the first hint of an executive council or cabinet. Outwardly, it looked more like responsible government, but when put to the test, it was seen that any changes from the previous order were minor. It was still Lieutenant Governor Joseph Royal's considered view that in expenditures from funds furnished by the federal government he had no responsibility to anyone outside that government.

When the Lieutenant Governor refused to submit the public accounts to the assembly, Haultain and his colleagues on the advisory committee resigned. No longer could they stand seeing the West being treated as though it were a colony of Canada. An alternative council was appointed, but it failed to win support from the assembly and was short-lived. There was a further administrative crisis, and then another election. But before voters went to the polls, the North West Territories Act was amended again, this time giving the assembly more spending authority, as Haultain had been demanding. Thereafter, the Lieutenant Governor would be able to authorize expenditures only upon the advice of the elected representatives. The change would make the council, of which Haultain was still the chairman, more like a cabinet and the chairman more like a premier.

Haultain knew what he wanted and what the country needed. He wanted a province, not two provinces which would necessitate two sets of legislative machinery when one would do. He wanted the natural resources turned over to the province or provinces, and he wanted provincial control over education. He did not favour the principle of separate schools.

The demand for provincial autonomy grew louder and louder. As the new century was ushered in on January 1, 1900, Premier Haultain was insisting that his territory was ready for provincial government. Soon after, in 1901, he submitted to Ottawa a working plan for the erection of a new province.

The Territories may, indeed, have been ready for provincial government, but Ottawa was not ready, not until 1905. Federal legislation to bring two new provinces into Confederation was introduced in the House of Commons by Prime Minister Wilfrid Laurier on February 21, 1905. By the terms of the act, there would be two provinces. There would be cash subsidies, but the Government of Canada would retain ownership of public lands.

It was the long-awaited action, although not exactly as Haultain wanted it. Nevertheless, it was not something to be thrown away. Haultain wrote to Laurier, expressing his disappointment in some features, but nothing of consequence came from the correspondence.

Debate in the House of Commons was long and bitter, but the bill's passage came on July 5, 1905, to take effect on September 1 of the same year. The new provinces, Saskatchewan and Alberta, were to have legislatures comprising 25 members each. Regina would be the capital of Saskatchewan and Edmonton the provisional capital of Alberta. The final decision about Alberta's capital would be left to its own legislature.

In the weeks following, G. H. V. Bulyea was appointed Lieutenant Governor of Alberta and A. E. Forget the Lieutenant Governor of Saskatchewan. September 1 would be the day for inauguration exercises in Alberta, but because Governor General Earl Grey and Prime Minister Wilfrid Laurier wished to be present for the ceremonies in both provinces, it became necessary to delay the Saskatchewan formalities until September 4. Consequently, the claim might be made that Alberta is senior to Saskatchewan by three days.

At both Edmonton and Regina, local people made the most of their celebrations. The Governor General and Prime Minister were there with top hats and broad smiles. There were parades, bands, cannon fire, and long speeches to make the two holidays the gayest the frontier country had experienced.

As inauguration formalities passed, politicians began preparations for the first elections and constitutional government. In Alberta, the Lieutenant Governor turned to A. C. Rutherford, Liberal member from Strathcona in the Territorial Assembly, and invited him to take the office of premier until an election could be conducted. In Saskatchewan, the corresponding call to become the first of the province's premiers went to Walter Scott, Regina journalist, who defeated Nicholas Flood Davin in the federal election of 1900. Haultain's friends, thinking that he should have been called, were both disappointed and angry, but the man who had guided territorial affairs through the years had learned to accept political fortunes and misfortunes philosophically.

In Saskatchewan's first election, held before the end of 1905, Walter Scott was returned with 16 seats. In Alberta, Rutherford won 23 out of the 25 constituencies.

As the Alberta Legislature met on March 15, 1906, one of its thorniest problems was in settling upon a location for the provincial capital. Calgary was determined to have it. Red Deer and Banff wanted it and advanced reasons why they should have it. Edmonton, having had it temporarily, had no intention of giving it up. There was a considerable amount of lobbying, and the controversy was bitter. Finally, when the question was put to a vote, Edmonton had the greater number of balloting friends in the legislature and won the decision over Calgary, with sixteen votes for Edmonton and eight for the southern city.

The road leading to responsible government was long and rough, but success was sweet. As for Haultain, the statesman of his time, he remained in public life for many years. He was the leader of the Opposition in Saskatchewan until 1912, then Chief Justice of that province, and ultimately, Sir Frederick Haultain.

The Shock of War

The rumble of guns from beyond the Atlantic in August 1914 signalled the beginning of World War I and shocked Canadians everywhere. At once, the lines separating the East from the West in the country disappeared; all was Canada, and the ensuing effort was a worthy one. The Canadian conduct was immediately like that of a responsible nation more than a colony.

Some young Canadians had a taste of war in South Africa a few years earlier and won high praise, but the fighting in Europe was different, terribly different; it was bloodier, longer, and more costly. In the end, there was hardly a family which did not mourn the loss of a father, son, or brother.

It had been known that Germany was arming with powerful weapons and a great fleet, but the knowledge failed to excite proper preparedness in other nations. Canadians, relying upon the British fleet, had done little beyond acquiring a couple of naval vessels in 1910 and opening a naval college in the next year. It was fashionable to make jokes about the Canadian navy. Bob Edwards informed readers of the famous *Eye Opener* that the two Canadian ships of war, *Rainbow* and *Niobe*, were not won in a raffle but were actually purchased for purposes of defence.

Quebec had shown opposition to anything which might lead to involvement in foreign wars, and Prime Minister Sir Wilfrid Laurier was obliged to tread cautiously. In the election of 1911, Canadian naval policy was attacked bitterly by some politicians who said it was too meagre to be of any practical value and by others who warned that it was enough to draw the country into international disputes.

Regardless of inadequacies in Canadian defence preparations prior to 1914, nobody could criticize the country's effort after Britain's declaration of war on August 4 of that year. France and Russia were already committed, and member countries of the British Empire responded quickly, leaving no doubt about sentiment for the Mother Country. Canada pledged aid to the limit of the country's resources and set about to making good its promises.

Canada's Minister of Militia, Sir Sam Hughes, brought spectacular energy to the raising of troops, and in seven weeks after the declaration of war, some 34,000 Canadian soldiers were on their way overseas, headed for trench warfare. Young men left farms, factories, mines, lumber woods, fishing fleets, and offices to enlist, and more and bigger contingents followed to confront the German military machine, the strongest and most devastating the world had known.

At Ypres, in April 1915, Canadians were attacked with poison gas, and the result in death and injury was terrible. But the line held, and the Germans were prevented from reaching the English Channel. Canadians saw action on several of the most terrifying fronts. There was Vimy Ridge, where one of the crucial battles of the war was fought, also one of the bloodiest and, according to students of military strategy, one of the most perfectly planned. Canadians attacked and took the Ridge of Passchendaele where the cost in lives and suffering again was high.

The record remained high. In 1918, the last year of the war, Canadian troops played their courageous part in the drive before Amiens and, on November 11, during the final hours of the long and awful struggle, they were among those who drove the Germans from Mons, where the British suffered their first defeat in 1914.

There was no Canadian airforce at that time, but some thousands of young men joined the British Air Force, demonstrating both skill and courage. Before the war was over, Canada had a navy deserving respect rather than levity. The naval role was mainly in combatting German submarines.

At home, the unity which characterized the onset of war did not last. The rate of voluntary enlistment dropped, and by 1916, the Government of Canada was obliged to consider conscription, to which a strong element in the province of Quebec objected vociferously. The political implications were obvious and the government was worried. In spite of opposition to it, the Military Service Bill was passed in August 1917. When a federal election was held later in that year, conscription was a leading issue. Most English-speaking voters supported Robert Borden's Union government, while most Quebec voters supported Laurier's Liberals, making for a most unfortunate rift in a country very conscious of the need for unity.

The war ended in victory, although the price was high and terrible: 60,000 Canadians dead, 200,000 wounded, and billions of dollars in national debt. But Canadians found reasons for pride mingled with their sorrow. Sacrifices had been made from highest motives and, for a country with a small population, an army of over 600,000, more than two-thirds going overseas, was a huge achievement. Even those who were not in uniform accepted challenges and made records in service.

It is never easy to find benefit in war, but World War I did seem to do something useful for the young country. The calls for food and industrial war materials stimulated Canadian production and the Canadian economy more than anything which went before. Agricultural production and export from the West made new records. Even more significant, the war effort aided Canada's graduation from colony to nation. In its new maturity, Canada was among the nations to sign the Peace Treaty, and then to become a responsible member of the League of Nations, upon which so much of mankind's hope for lasting peace rested.

War came only nine years after the provinces of Saskatchewan and Alberta were created, but the West as a whole responded with its full national share of production and effort. In the last year of the war, western production, including 435 million bushels of wheat, oats, and barley, was more like that of a seasoned partner in nationhood.

The Birth of the Wheat Pools

More and more, wheat was seen as the very lifeblood of the big country stretching from Winnipeg to the Rockies. When the crops were good, the economy was good; when the crops failed, there was depression. Men on city streets watched the yields and the price of wheat with almost as much feeling as if they were growers. The marketing of wheat became an increasingly favourite topic of conversation.

War set the stage for the most dramatic events in marketing the western crop. For years, farmers mistrusted speculative grain selling as carried on through the Winnipeg Grain Exchange. Wheat prices were generally low in the autumn, but farmers could not wait for markets to improve. It had happened too often that they sold their wheat soon after harvest when farm debts were coming due, only to see prices rising and speculators getting rich. On various occasions, producer groups asked for firmer controls, but governments had no wish to become involved, at least not until wartime wheat prices threatened to run wild.

Anxious to check inflation and rising living costs, the federal government appointed a board of grain supervisors to handle deliveries from the crops of 1917 and 1918. Grain Exchange trading was suspended, and farmers sold at prices fixed by the board. To handle the crop of 1919, the government appointed the first Canadian Wheat Board, with full authority to buy, sell, and set prices.

Farmers fancied the Wheat Board, which was really a country-wide compulsory pool. Upon delivery to the Board, they would receive an initial payment, and later, a final payment based on the total return from the year's sales. With the Board in operation, producers knew that they were not supporting speculators and that returns would represent an average of the best prices obtainable. For one reason or another, however, the federal government refused to extend the life of the Wheat Board, and in August 1920, the Winnipeg Grain Exchange came back into operation, again drawing the criticism of wheat growers across the plains.

After the resumption of Exchange trading, prices remained strong for a time and then fell to less than a dollar per bushel late in 1923. Growers who wanted another wheat board watched with increasing annoyance as they saw their income falling. They were numerous enough to do something for themselves; if the government would not meet their request, there was always the possibility of a giant cooperative with the pooling feature of a wheat board. Why not?

Since farm neighbours had always worked together with mutual benefit, farmers knew a considerable amount about cooperation. Leaders had talked about the principles which brought success to the cooperating English weavers at Rochdale. There had been various cooperative undertakings among Canadian pioneers. The earliest may have been in Nova Scotia in 1765, and in the West, a consumer cooperative was started at Winnipeg at least as early as 1885. Indeed, the Territorial Grain Growers' Association, organized in 1901, and the cooperative elevator companies were other good examples.

Farm leaders encouraged discussion about something big in the cooperative marketing of grain, and by the summer of 1923, when all hope of obtaining another wheat board for the year had disappeared, the prairie farmers were in a proper mood for action.

Supporting the idea of self-help were leaders like Henry Wise Wood, President of the United Farmers of Alberta, and James Alexander McPhail of Saskatchewan. It was already late in the season when Aaron Sapiro of California was invited to the prairies to tell of his experiences with producer cooperatives in that state. Sapiro's oratory electrified his Canadian listeners, and notwithstanding the lateness of the season, a decision was made to attempt a crash-type campaign for grower contracts, to get promises from the farmers that they would deliver all their wheat for a period of five years.

Saskatchewan workers set out to obtain contracts on six million acres of wheat in a 12-day campaign, and when they found it practically impossible to reach the goal in time remaining, they resolved to postpone the program until the next year.

Alberta's objective was to cover 50 per cent of the total wheat acreage in the province with delivery contracts, allowing the period from August 20 to September 5 for the campaign. At the end of the period, the signed contracts came somewhat short of the objective, but with 26,211 farmers having formally committed 45 per cent of Alberta's total wheat acreage, the response seemed to justify proceeding with the pooling plan. To the credit of the bold leaders of the movement, the Alberta Wheat Pool marketed 34 million bushels of wheat in its first year of operation. The price obtained for the year's volume of sales was $1.01 per bushel, basis No. 1 N. (Northern), Fort William. Handling costs were kept down, and best of all, there was a price stability which appealed strongly to most farmers.

Publicity Department, Alberta Wheat Pool

One of the many elevators owned by the Alberta Wheat Pool. Co-operative pooling became an important feature in western wheat farming in 1923.

Starting earlier in 1924, Saskatchewan and Manitoba obtained the necessary contract signatures and brought the respective provincial pools into being. In July 1924, leaders from the three provincial pools met and set up the Central Selling Agency to handle sales for all member bodies. Saskatchewan's McPhail was named chairman, with Alberta's Wood as vice-chairman, and Manitoba's C. H. Burnell as secretary.

The pools did well, acquiring experience and elevators. Everything pointed to continuing success until the unforeseen setback which came with the stock market crash of October 1929.

Based on their record of five or six years of successful selling, pool leaders were showing increasing confidence in their methods, and on the incoming crop of 1929, they offered an initial price of one dollar per bushel. There was no reason to believe the administration was being any more reckless than in former years. Even the banks loaning money for such payments sensed no particular danger or risk and marketing was taking the usual course when, suddenly, the bottom seemed to fall out of the stock markets, the wheat market included.

Perhaps more notice should have been taken of certain international signs. The world situation with regard to wheat was changing, and surpluses were bigger, whether they were recognized or not. Buyers were more indifferent, and when prices started to fall, they fell faster and further than anybody would have considered even remotely possible.

When prices reached $1.15 per bushel, the pool bankers might have forced the sale of stocks on hand in order to protect their loans, but this was prevented when the three provincial governments agreed to guarantee the banks against loss. In this way, the pools were able to continue holding their grain in anticipation of the price improvement everybody felt sure would come very soon. It seemed inconceivable that wheat prices would go still lower.

Nevertheless, holding brought no benefit; instead, it brought more losses and more frustrations because world prices continued to fall. Wheat was becoming ever harder to sell, even at those prices which were well below the initial payment made by the pools to grower members. Actually, much of the year's crop was sold at prices well below a dollar per bushel. As a consequence, the provincial pools ended up with big debts to the provincial governments: $12,500,000 in the case of Saskatchewan, $5,500,000 in Alberta, and $3,300,000 in Manitoba.

Pool critics found it difficult to hide their satisfaction. They were sure the farmers would now quit cooperative marketing and let wheat return to the Exchange.

Some of the criticism directed at the pools might have been justified. Wheat men with more experience in marketing might have avoided some of the pitfalls, but the wheat pools were not to disappear, not by any means.

The period of marketing trouble did not end quickly. In 1930, the situation was no better than it had been in the previous year, and after the pools had offered 70 cents per bushel as initial payment, they discovered that even that modest amount was too much. The price trend was still downward, the market was still lifeless, and the initial price payment had to be revised to 50 cents.

Pool policy had to be changed. Some growers called for compulsory pools with all growers in them; others wanted to be released from their pooling contracts. It was a trying time for those who were attempting to keep the huge cooperatives alive.

With pressure from banks and governments, the general management of the pools was turned over to John I. McFarland, formerly of the Alberta Pacific Grain Company. McFarland was an able and experienced grain man, and he made some important changes in his determination to spare the wheat producers from further losses. He closed the pools' overseas selling office and sold pool wheat on the Winnipeg Grain Exchange. It was humiliating to the cooperatives and their friends, but the leaders stood resolute to make the pools live again.

Since the pools faced the prospect of nothing better than 35 cents per bushel initial payment, and that on the basis of Fort William, the growers were released from the terms of their delivery contracts following a meeting in the summer of 1931. Thereafter they could sell where they chose, but they were urged to continue, as far as possible, to use wheat pool elevators.

The revised plan marked a completely new day for the three provincial pools. With the return of a Canadian Wheat Board, which the farmers continued to request, the pools became handling agencies with extensive interests in elevators, both country and terminal. From the near-failures in the early years of depression came new successes. The Canadian Wheat Board, functioning as a government-operated pool, relieved the provincial pools of the kind of risk which led to the reverses of 1929. The debts to provincial governments were paid, and the pools, with ambitious elevator programs, flourished again and became forces of great influence in the western agricultural community.

The Dry and Depressing Thirties

No one who lived in the West during the thirties could possibly forget the hardship and the disappointment he underwent. As if financial depression ushered in with the stock market crash in October 1929 were not enough to try human patience to the limit, Nature inflicted a series of drought years, the worst that old timers could recall, and the result was bitter indeed. Excluding periods when the country was engaged in war, it was the blackest period in western Canadian history.

The impact of the depression was felt in all parts of Canada and even around the world, but there were those added hardships from drought which made life in the West particularly disagreeable, almost unbearable. It was not surprising that thousands of people left the country at that time.

Nor did the market failure which brought tragic losses to wheat pools in 1929 and 1930 correct itself in a hurry. Agricultural products did not strike bottom until 1932 and 1933. In 1933, yearling steers selling at the Saskatchewan Feeder Show, in Moose Jaw, averaged $2.75 per hundred and in 1934, $2.35 per hundred. By 1938, the average price for yearling steers at that show was still only $5.20.

Wheat prices struck their lowest point on Friday, December 16, 1932. On a market demoralized by overseas indifference, No. 1 N. wheat traded at 39⅜ cents per bushel, basis Fort William. Back in prairie communities, the net price to producers was, inevitably, considerably less. At Edmonton, on that date, No. 2 N. wheat would bring no more than 17½ cents per bushel, while No. 3 C.W. oats would command 4½ cents per bushel and No. 4 C.W. barley, 8 cents. Where still bigger freight charges applied, as at Dawson Creek, on the British Columbia side of the Peace River area, the same grains and grades were bringing 10½ cents, 1 cent, and 2 cents per bushel respectively.

If dockage rates were heavy, prices to the farmers would be even lower. It was not difficult to understand stories told of farmers selling thin cattle or low grade grains and finding that, instead of receiving a payment, they were being billed for a net balance because the products sold had failed to bring enough to pay for transportation and other charges against them.

Farmers were not the only ones in trouble. More and more men became unemployed. Many of those without work rode freight trains back and forth across the country. Bankruptcy was widespread, and most people who were self-employed found themselves spending more than they were making, slowly going broke.

The prolonged drought began about the same time as the depression but did not reach its climax until 1937, the year it didn't rain, as many people recalled it. Nature, it seemed, had forsaken the prairies. Indians were sure it indicated the Great Spirit's displeasure at the white man's greedy haste to exploit the land, forests, and game.

Western climate was an extremely variable thing at the best of times, and dry land farmers knew that they were completely at the mercy of the weather. Crops had to have moisture. According to experimental farm studies, it required 60 tons of water to produce one bushel of wheat. When Saskatchewan produced more than four times as much wheat in 1966 as in 1961, the chief reason could be found in the difference in the amount of water available.

Long-time weather history showed fairly prolonged spells of drought recurring from time to time but not with any apparent pattern or regularity. A series of dry years occurred during the eighties of last century; six out of seven years between 1883 and 1889 were below average in moisture. But the drought of the recent thirties was more severe than any which preceded it during the white man's stay on the plains. What people saw in 1937 was a practical demonstration of possible extremes within the Palliser Triangle. Markets recovered measurably from the levels of 1932 and 1933, but a better price for wheat was poor comfort for a man who had nothing to sell because of drought and grasshoppers.

The rains needed in June and July did not come, and every wind managed to whip up a dust storm. Dry days were trying enough, but nothing was more depressing than the "black blizzards" which robbed fields of their best soil. There was the almost constant torment of a person being struck in the face by soil, or inhaling it, or finding it changing the colour of his clothing. It was impossible to get away from the airborne silt which found its way into homes to settle on furniture, dishes, and bedspreads. Dust made it dangerous to be on the roads, and men doing field work with horses complained about the dust being so thick at times that they could not see their teams.

Windblown soil piled up in roadside ditches and on headlands. Implements left in fields were known to be buried in a day or two, and fences were often so covered that cattle walked over them. It was difficult to see anything entertaining in the situation, but to their credit, farmers did not lose their sense of humour. As related at Swift Current, a town resident fainted during a church service, and since there was no water handy, his friends threw a bucket of dust on him and saw him revive. A farmer explaining the density of dust over his fields said he saw a gopher digging a hole ten feet above the ground. They told about seven-year-old frogs that had never learned to swim and a twelve-year-old boy who had seen a picture of a five-dollar bill but had never seen a real one.

Sloughs and some lakes went dry in 1937; most plants withered. Only cactus and Russian thistles grew normally, and livestock as well as crops suffered. Much of the West took on the appearance of a desert. For Saskatchewan, the province to suffer most, 14 million acres of wheatland returned only 36 million bushels of grain, an average of about 2½ bushels per acre. Barley averaged 4.7 bushels per acre and oats 5.1 bushels.

On one central Saskatchewan farm for which there happened to be precise records, the 500 cultivated acres normally furnishing feed for livestock yielded nothing more than 200 loads of Russian thistles. Drought could not destroy resourcefulness, however, and the unappetizing thistles were made to serve a purpose. Some of the unattractive roughage was put up as hay, some as silage, and some was cooked, but regardless of treatment, the feed was still repulsive, still high in fibre, still about as unpalatable as Epsom salts. The amazing fact was that most of the livestock on that farm survived the winter. "About as nourishing as old straw and a bit more appetizing than barbed wire," was the way a stockman described his Russian thistle hay.

In meeting the emergency of 1937, both federal and provincial governments undertook to remove large numbers of cattle and other livestock from the farms and import feed for the remaining minimum numbers. Nearly half a million cattle were taken from the drought area, some for slaughter, some for eastern feedlots, and some to be carried to government pasture near Carberry, Manitoba. At the same time, 488,000 tons of hay were shipped to needy districts in Saskatchewan and Alberta. Federal government feed and fodder sent to Saskatchewan alone in one year cost over $10 million.

Furnishing food for people in the stricken area was no less difficult. In a big section of prairie country, it seemed that about everybody was on relief. Organizations in the East and elsewhere heard the call for assistance and responded with carloads of food: fruit from British Columbia, vegetables from Ontario, dried codfish from the Maritimes, and potatoes from various parts. The government of Saskatchewan distributed some 550 carloads of potatoes.

Nearly all of the Midwest felt the dull blow from drought in that year, and a hundred thousand people abandoned farm lands on the prairies, some to seek fortunes in the cities, others to find situations in the wooded and park districts to the north.

Pessimism was almost as thick as the dust hanging over prairie fields, and even editors indulged in gloomy predictions. Some writers suggested that the western wheat economy had ended forever, saying that the climate had changed and the soil had lost its productiveness. One of them went so far as to urge the federal government to bring back the buffalo herds and give them the freedom and grazing they enjoyed before the settlers came.

Any way it was seen, 1937 was a memorable year, but it passed and the outlook changed. At the outbreak of World War II, western farmers heard a call for more food, and almost at once, Nature was more generous with her rainfall. Better crops were harvested; better prices were realized; debts were adjusted; and the scars from erosion did not appear as bad. The experiences from the dry and dirty thirties were rather quickly forgotten, perhaps too quickly. It should not be forgotten that the extremes of drought which brought poverty and suffering in the thirties can come again, and probably will.

Another World War

For the second time in 25 years, Canada's people found themselves plunged into world war, and the West, no less than the East, responded with men, money, and materials. Again the entire outlook seemed to change, even the weather. As if born in the clouds of war, rains fell more abundantly on prairie farmlands to end the long spell of drought, and wartime demand for certain farm products helped to dull the memory of those years when eggs sold at four cents per dozen and barley was hardly worth hauling to the elevator.

With its membership in the League of Nations, Canada had been relying upon collective security. It was fine in theory, but in one test after another, the League failed to halt aggression, such as during the Japanese invasion of China in 1931 and Mussolini's attack upon Ethiopia in 1935. Worse still for the Western World, Hitler was building up the mightiest war machine of all time in Germany. After ignoring warnings and breaking treaties by occupying the Rhineland, he sent his armies into Austria, then Czechoslovakia and Poland. Britain felt compelled to intervene and declared war. Canada followed on September 10, 1939, declaring "a state of war with the German Reich". Differing from 1914, it was now Canada's right to make such a declaration on her own behalf.

At that time, Germany was the only nation really prepared for a gigantic struggle. Canada's forces were meagre indeed: army, navy, and air force personnel totalled fewer than 10,000. Again the Canadian people declared their determination to support the war effort with all the resources they could command. Warfare had changed greatly, but it was still costly and cruel. It was perfectly clear that more of the combat would be in the air. Ground forces would still be important and the naval tasks no smaller than in World War I. Actually, Canada's new naval strength was to be many times greater than in the other war. At the same time, the air force would be new, big, and impressive.

Canadian troops, ultimately numbering 600,000, carried the brunt of the ill-fated assault upon the French coast at Dieppe in 1942 and did their full share in the more successful invasion of Normandy, the campaigns in Belgium, Holland, Africa, Sicily, and Italy, and the climactic defeat of German armies in 1944 and 1945. The Canadian navy, as it gained strength, assumed a big role in keeping the sea lanes open for shipping, while one of Canada's most conspicuous parts was through the Royal Canadian Air Force and the British Commonwealth Air Training Plan, thanks to which 131,583 men from 14 countries obtained their training for combat under Canadian skies.

While the war continued overseas, leaders on the home front faced delicate issues like conscription. More and more men were needed. How were they to be secured without conscription and how was conscription to be introduced without serious threat to national unity? These were the most perplexing political questions of the time. Prime Minister Mackenzie King had given assurance that conscription for overseas service would not be adopted, but in a provincial election early in the war period, people in Quebec were frightened by warnings issued in emotional terms that the federal government was soon to force conscription upon them and take their sons to war. A nation engaged in a life and death struggle could not stand internal division. Naturally, federal leaders were anxious to avoid the danger.

From sources outside Quebec came demands for more vigorous prosecution of the war, and conscription was a bitter issue in the federal election of

1940. In spite of this, Mackenzie King's Liberal government was overwhelmingly successful, and the matter of conscription seemed to be settled to the satisfaction of those who opposed it, at least for the moment; however, it was not settled for long. The government came under pressure to do more to assure victory, and this led to a compromise measure, the National Resources Mobilization Act, which practically allowed for conscription of people for service within Canada but not for service outside of the country.

National registration followed and all adults carried registration cards, but as the war continued, the need for conscription for overseas' duty became more evident, and the government at Ottawa was obliged, once again, to do something. With Quebec and the rest of the country holding different views, what could be done that would achieve the purpose without splitting the Dominion with dissension? Mackenzie King deferred as long as he dared under the circumstances and then, notwithstanding previous assurances that conscription would not be adopted, he appealed through a plebiscite for the public's approval to his resorting to conscription if it were considered necessary. As it turned out, the majority of English-speaking Canadians voted to give approval, the majority of French-speaking Canadians against it.

Even the King cabinet was divided on the conscription issue, with Col. J. L. Ralston, Minister of Defence, being the leading proponent for compulsory military service. The manpower shortage was becoming more serious, and Col. Ralston's convictions stiffened. The Prime Minister, still doing all in his power to avoid the national rupture which would almost certainly accompany conscription, dropped Ralston as Minister of National Defence and named General A. G. L. McNaughton in his place. McNaughton, a native of Moosomin, Saskatchewan, failed to gain a seat in the House of Commons, however, and also failed in obtaining the men needed by the services through voluntary enlistment.

The time came, late in the war, when Prime Minister Mackenzie King and his government were obliged to implement conscription, whatever the political consequences. But the obvious delay and reluctance on the part of the government tended to minimize objections from Quebec, and before long the war ended.

In the meantime, wartime demands led to greatly increased industrial activity across the country, with more output from factories, farms, mines, and forests. The economy gathered momentum. British Columbia furnished more lumber and more minerals than ever before. The prairies, even with the shortage of help, increased agricultural production by at least 25 per cent. The increase was not in wheat but in feed grains and human foods like bacon, cheese, dried milk, beef, and eggs.

World War II, unlike World War I, did not create an immediate increase in the demand for wheat. Actually, the second world war resulted in the loss of most of Canada's traditional wheat customers. Only the United Kingdom continued to take Canadian wheat in quantity, and with improved crops, the wheat surplus mounted to 480 million bushels on August 1, 1941. The federal government offered wheat acreage reduction payments as high as $4 per acre, but the surplus continued to grow, until it reached 595 million bushels on August 1, 1943. Although wheat sales remained low, Britain came to depend upon Canada for bacon and other foods of animal origin. Farmers in all provinces geared themselves to produce what Allied consumers wanted and needed, but the most spectacular increase in "bacon for Britain" was in the West where feed grains were plentiful and farmers, unable to sell all their wheat, were glad to help the war effort while doing something for themselves.

The fact was that in the latter years of the war pigs were being kept on western farms where such stock had never been seen before. In the face of the shortage of manpower, farm boys and girls assumed responsibility for the care of pigs. Even urban residents were keeping pigs on the outskirts of towns and cities. Lawyers talked about the pig crop and church ministers cut short their Sunday sermons because they had pigs to feed.

The war ended late in 1945 and Canadians took stock, mourned their 42,000 dead and 53,000 wounded, and counted cash costs coming close to $20 billion dollars. They also came out of the war recognizing a clearer role in world affairs. Thereafter, they would exercise greater interpretative responsibilities between the United States and the United Kingdom and speak more clearly in world councils. Canada seemed to emerge as a leader among the smaller powers, and when the United Nations was born at San Francisco, Canada's voice was more convincing than it had ever been before.

8 The Canadian West of Today

Education for the New West

From the one-room school of other years to the modern structure seen today; from the slates and battered, outdated textbooks of the past to the expensive audio-visual aids and well-stocked libraries of the present; from the earnest but often ill-trained teachers of frontier times to the knowledgeable professionals of today, the story of education in the West has been one of progress, mirroring the economic advancement of the provinces themselves.

The first actual schools in the West were located in what is now Manitoba. There is some evidence of a school being opened on the banks of Red River in 1815, but credit for the original venture generally goes to Father Provencher who, with two companions, opened a school in the autumn of 1818. Priests and nuns were particularly active in setting up schools and, by 1872, there were 17 Roman Catholic schools in the Red River colony. Under Rev. John West, the Anglicans embarked upon a school-building program in 1820, and the Presbyterians had their own school in 1849, an institution which was to form the foundation for the College of Manitoba. Thus it was religious groups which initiated and implemented education in this area. Indeed, it was not until 1871, a year after the province was created, that a system of public education was introduced.

In the area marked later by the provinces of Saskatchewan and Alberta, the story was much the same, with church missionaries serving as educational pioneers. Beginning in 1836, isolated outposts of education were established around Fort Edmonton. The number of schools grew rapidly after the coming of railroads, but the North West Territories officials did very little in assuming the costs. It was only when provincial status was granted that the governments assumed the major financial responsibilities.

The difficulties encountered by those who pioneered in education were many and varied. Neither frontier parents nor pupils showed much enthusiasm for regular school attendance, and a buffalo hunt was always enough to empty the classroom. A teacher at Whitefish Lake, in present-day Alberta, concluded that his only hope of keeping in contact with his pupils was in following them on buffalo hunts, just as they were following parents. The sceptic will enquire, quite naturally, if the teacher's motives were dictated solely by concern for his pupils or if he wanted a good excuse to be riding with the hunters.

In British Columbia, the first schools were established at Victoria in 1849, when the Hudson's Bay Company undertook to provide education for children of its employees. Then, although church missionaries were active on Vancouver Island and the mainland, the main form of educational service came through the government-sponsored colonial schools. The first of these was set up at Victoria in 1852, with others at Nanaimo and Craigflower one year later. More schools followed and, by 1856, the authorities even appointed an Inspector of Schools, Rev. E. Cridge.

On the mainland, educational opportunities were presented more slowly. The first school was established at New Westminster in 1862 by Rev. R. Jamieson. Within three years, the mainland had five colonial schools. When British Columbia entered Confederation, the new province had a total of 15 schools and an enrolment of nearly a thousand pupils.

Two factors appeared to stand out in respect to British Columbia's early attempts to provide education: the first was the relatively advanced state of the schools at the time the province was formed, and the second was that the government rather than religious bodies was most active from the beginning. In any case, after joining Confederation, education became the responsibility of the provincial governments. Education Acts were passed, laying down conditions under which education was to be administered. It was not simple, for the problems were many: religious, language, administrative, and financial. There was also the question of teacher training. It was quite remarkable that all the western provinces had worked out similar school systems by the end of the first decade in the new century, given the bitter controversies of the period.

When one notes that by 1912 the opening of new school districts in the West was about as commonplace as the arrival of branch line mail trains, it is easy to see that education was progressing in spite of its problems.

It was still the day of the one-room country school of which many older Canadians have fond memories. It was the school to which they walked from one to three miles five mornings a week and from which they walked the same distance when school was dismissed. Known familiarly as the "schoolhouse", its architecture was often ugly and its facilities limited, but it served its purpose well. Behind it was the simple stable for the benefit of a few pupils fortunate enough to have saddle or driving horses for their transportation. Flanking the stable were the two familiar toilet structures served only by well beaten paths.

Inside that typical school were rows of crudely constructed desks, generally one row for each grade. The lady teacher, who had from 40 to 60 pupils distributed among eight grades, was left with very little time to worry about the small size of her salary or the large number of bachelor farmers trying to outbid each other for her attention.

There was no tap water, but there was a tin pail with a dipper and basin at the rear of the room. The pupils took turns to replenish the water from a pump over the school well. After the summer holidays, when no demands were made upon the well, it yielded only stagnant water, sufficiently repulsive that even the over-driven school ponies refused it until thirst became unbearable.

In cold winter weather, no amount of firing was enough to ensure against a crust of ice on the water pail. Under such circumstances, many pupils sat in their overcoats all day. As a winter assignment carrying a cash reward of three dollars per month, one of the older boys came early each morning to remove the ashes and start the fire in either the furnace or heater. By the time the other pupils arrived, there was, at least, a place where near-frozen fingers and toes could be warmed up.

Serving as an institution of learning by day, the school was the meeting place for the local debating society on Friday evenings, Church School sessions on Sunday afternoons, and the headquarters for the community baseball team whenever needed. It was a lowly structure, but from the point of view of service in the community, its contribution was truly great.

Expansion of education in the years prior to 1900 was mainly at the elementary level, but with the rapid growth of the population in the first decades of the new century, greater emphasis was placed on secondary and high school education. This rapid expansion was brought to an abrupt halt by the disastrous effects of the depression of the thirties which saw a decrease in both pupil and teacher population. Moreover, recovery from this educational slump was slow. Even in 1949, the school population in Saskatchewan had not recovered to the 1931 level. In the next two decades, however, education came to figure more vitally in the spending budgets of all western provinces, with the result that in the 1964-65 year, the four western provinces had a total of 6,846 schools, 51,415 teachers, 1,267,254 pupils, and education budgets adding up to $469,628,000.

Simon Fraser University looking northwest. This is one of the youngest of the western universities.

In the years after World War II, a population drift toward the cities resulted in financial inequality among taxpayers for the support of their schools. This, combined with the relative shortage of teachers, was instrumental in bringing about the larger administrative units or school districts. All four provinces developed this centralization of educational authority to one degree or another.

Nowhere was the new emphasis upon education more noticeable than in the growth of western universities. The University of Manitoba founded in 1877, the University of Saskatchewan in 1907, the University of Alberta in 1908, and the University of British Columbia in 1908 were all started on the prevailing theory of a single university per province. It was believed that each of the western provinces could be adequately served by a single university and that more than one would be an extravagance, but a glance at the universities of Centennial Year would show the four western provinces with no fewer than 10 such institutions. The additional six were products of the sixties.

Education reached out into other spheres as well to include Vocational Guidance Schools, Schools for the Handicapped, Technological and Junior Colleges, Agricultural Schools, and Night Schools for adults, all reflecting the new demands for educational advantages.

This expansion serves to illustrate that education in western Canada had a spectacular growth after a slow beginning. The rapid growth during the present century seems to be in line with the transformation of the western provinces from purely rural communities to the modern and complex society of recent years.

Agriculture, The Mother Industry

For 75 years after the first wheat was shipped out, agriculture was not only the Midwest's primary industry but it was, for all practical purposes, the only industry. The prospect of growing and selling wheat was the main attraction for settlers in the first place, and the returns from wheat paid for railroads, highways, schools, and services which marked the transformation from frontier to modern community.

Manitoba, Saskatchewan, and Alberta together possessed 75 per cent of the arable soil of Canada, surely the most precious of all the resources. It was to be the source of Canada's bread and the biggest contributor to the nation's agricultural exports which were valued at $1,702,017,000 in 1964.

The discovery of oil at Leduc in 1947 changed many things and provided new sources of income. In the industrial adjustments which followed, agriculture lost some of its exclusiveness but did not lose its supreme importance to the nation and the world.

All the while, agriculture itself was changing in a spectacular way. Here, indeed, was agricultural revolution. Research, travel, and education resulted in new and progressive ideas in the rural communities. Farmers were not satisfied with old methods, and practices followed on a modern mechanized western farm came to bear only a slight resemblance to those in vogue at the beginning of the present century when most units were of the quarter-section or half-section size, and field work was performed exclusively by horses or oxen.

A modern, high-speed tractor on rubber tires could make a four-horse team pulling a two-furrow plow, ten-foot seed drill, or seven-foot binder seem slow and totally inadequate. A self-propelled combine, operated by one man and threshing as it advanced across a grain field, would appear dramatically more efficient than the old stationary threshing machine requiring a crew of from 8 to 28 workers. A modern milking machine, allowing one man to handle three or four times as many dairy cows as when the job was performed by hand, represented the kind of technical advance which could change an industry.

Understandably, such changes meant a greatly increased output per man in agriculture. While a representative farmer of the pioneer period was concerned mainly with producing food for members of his own family, a single worker, using the equipment and aids of 1967, could produce enough food for himself and 30 or 35 other people. It was an indication of the improved efficiency brought to agriculture, especially agriculture in the western farming community.

The changes and improvements in methods were so great that fewer people were needed to man the farms. Although Canada's total population increased, farm population decreased almost as sharply. Farms became bigger and fewer. Canadian farms in 1871 averaged only 98 acres in size and three-quarters of the country's population lived on them. In 1966, the average was 405 acres per farm and less than one-eighth of the Canadian people lived on them. The trend toward bigger farms was even more evident in the West, where farms were already big, than in the East. The average for western farms changed from 402 acres in 1941 to roughly 700 acres in 1966.

As for farm numbers, the Canadian total reached a peak of over 700,000 in 1941 and then, without any decrease in the total area under cultivation, the number declined to 276,835 commercial farms in 1966.

It was most significant that, nothwithstanding the decrease in farm numbers, total production increased greatly. Thanks to improved methods and favourable weather, western Canada's biggest crops were harvested after 1962, when the depletion of plant foods due to continued use of fields might have been expected to exert the opposite effect.

Improved methods took many shapes. Commercial fertilizers, rarely used in the pioneer period, were adopted with profitable results. Soils showing at least a measure of exhaustion after decades of cropping were responding to the application of plant foods, mainly nitrogen and phosphate. With the greater use of new cultivating tools instead of plows, farmers not only gained better control over drifting soil, but managed to reduce the time required for working land.

Western farmers continued to be heavy purchasers of machinery. The sales of farm equipment and implements for all of Canada in 1964, at wholesale prices, totalled $380,132,700. Of this total, Saskatchewan farmers accounted for $110,985,200, or almost 30 per cent. Purchases in the four western provinces, a quarter of a billion dollars worth of machinery, represented over 65 per cent of the national total.

Prairie farm rehabilitation and irrigation were important contributors to the new western agriculture. The former, backed by the Prairie Farm

P.F.R.A., Canada Department of Agriculture

A farm pond in Saskatchewan; one of the thousands created with assistance from the Prairie Farm Rehabilitation Act (P.F.R.A.).

Rehabilitation Act of 1935, began as a federal government attempt to aid in restoring western agriculture after the near-crippling reverses created by drought, drifting soil, and deplorable markets during the thirties. In its original form, P.F.R.A. was limited to Alberta, Saskatchewan, and Manitoba, but it was later extended to include British Columbia.

Conservation measures took various forms, and the record for the first 30 years showed 75 community pastures brought into operation and 4,732 irrigation projects, 76,732 dugouts, and 9,416 dams completed with P.F.R.A. assistance. Some of the dams and irrigation schemes were monumental undertakings, such as the South Saskatchewan River Project sponsored jointly by the federal and Saskatchewan governments and officially opened in July 1967.

The greatest progress with irrigation was in Alberta, where river water originating high in the foothills and mountains and the general topography were especially favourable. Alberta expected to have a million acres under the ditches, and Saskatchewan and British Columbia could look to the day when each would have about half a million acres of cropland enjoying the added protection provided by irrigation water.

Many of the risks which proved so disastrous in the thirties were lessened, thanks to improved techniques, crop insurance as administered by federal and provincial governments, and a better use of irrigation water. Rust-resistant varieties of grains helped to remove another threat to crops, and studies in weather modification gave hope for success in preventing losses from hail.

Crop insurance coverage in 1966 amounted to $52,000,000 and was shared by 24,500 farmers. With the federal government paying administration costs and 20 per cent of premiums, 25 per cent from 1967 onward, interest on the part of farmers was growing annually.

A degree of agricultural specialization was always in evidence in the West. Saskatchewan was unchallenged as Canada's leading wheat province, and her production in the big wheat year of 1963 was two-thirds of the Canadian total. Alberta could claim to be Canada's biggest producer of meats, ranking first among the provinces in beef, mutton, and lamb, second in pork, and third in poultry meats. British Columbia, although short of farmland, was second only to Ontario in fruit production. Indeed, the Okanagan Valley, where Thomas Ellis planted the first apple trees in 1874, is considered one of the world's best areas for fruits.

Still using 1963 figures, the four western provinces produced 97½ per cent of the Canadian total for wheat, 68 per cent of the oats, 97 per cent of the barley, and 100 per cent of the rapeseed. And as of the first of June in the same year, the western provinces had 54 per cent of all Canada's cattle, 56 per cent of the sheep, 38 per cent of the pigs, and 37 per cent of all poultry, meaning hens, turkeys, ducks, and geese. Milk production for the year showed 25 per cent of it as being produced in the West.

The figures should effectively contradict any remaining impressions that western farmers are strictly grain producers. Often, in other years, they heard eastern critics call them "wheat miners". Whatever justification there may have been for such aspersion, diversification of agriculture has made great strides in recent decades. Surviving critics should be reminded that if all western livestock were divided evenly among all the 154,712 commercial farms reported in 1966, each farm would have five milk cows, 40 other cattle, 13 pigs, five sheep, and 224 poultry, altogether enough to ensure a sizable program of morning and evening chores.

There were still those western operators who would classify as grain farmers, some of them being non-residents for a big part of each year, but most of those occupying western land were mixed farmers in the true sense. Although much was heard about trends toward large, factory-type farms, there was reason to believe that the owner-operator or family-type of farm would continue to be the principal and most enduring unit in western agriculture.

The Fishing Industry Survives

The first record of Canada's potential in the fishing industry was made by the Italian-born John Cabot, who sailed under the English flag in 1497. He reported seeing more fish in the water of the Grand Banks off the coast of Newfoundland than he had ever witnessed before, saying that the ocean there was so teeming with fish that they could be caught in baskets let down from the ship. In 1778, Captain James Cook, a distinguished officer and navigator with the Royal Navy, visited the North Pacific and was similarly impressed by the abundance of fish from Nootka north to the Bering Sea. Then Captain John Palliser, in making his celebrated survey of the buffalo country, was most enthusiastic about fish resources in lakes and rivers, convinced that the ever-available supply of fish would be the settler's best guarantee against starvation.

With great wealth in fish being drawn from two oceans and the world's biggest complex of freshwater lakes and rivers, both to the east and west, Canada is rich in fishing resources. An annual Canadian catch of roughly two billion pounds has to be seen as a great national asset. How is that catch divided between salt and fresh water? In 1963, the saltwater catch was valued at $244,000,000 and the freshwater catch at $20,000,000.

Inevitably, the industry differs greatly from province to province, but the West inherited a reasonable share of the resource. Fishing as a freshwater enterprise is important to the three midwestern provinces, but it is still small when compared with the extensive saltwater operations as conducted in British Columbia where it ranks as one of the four leading industries, employing approximately 20,000 fishermen and related workers. The value of fish landings in British Columbia in 1966 was about $59,000,000, compared with $47,000,000 in Nova Scotia, $26,000,000 in Newfoundland, and $11,000,000 in New Brunswick.

Salmon is by far the most important fish in British Columbia operations, followed by herring and halibut. Together, the three kinds account for 90 per cent of the total value of the annual harvest.

Long before white men came upon the scene, West Coast Indians speared salmon, ate them fresh or smoked, and relied upon them as much as the prairie Indians depended upon buffalo. The Hudson's Bay Company began using salmon for trade purposes and, in 1835, shipped out 4,000 barrels of salt-cured fish, but it was not until two years after Confederation that canning was started at Annieville, beside the Lower Fraser

River. Thereafter, interest grew rapidly as indicated by the increase in size of pack from 67,387 cases, at 48 pounds per case, in 1871, to 1,247,212 cases in 1901 when there were nearly 100 canneries in operation in the province. Canada became one of the four leading producers in the world. Although the United States and Japan drew heavily upon Pacific salmon, these countries cooperated through the International Convention for the High Seas Fisheries of the North Pacific to regulate fishing in such a way that yield might be sustained at the highest possible level.

One of the finest examples of effective cooperation in international circles is the Pacific Salmon Fisheries Convention, instituted to protect the multimillion dollar sockeye salmon industry of the Fraser River system. The administering commission was appointed in 1937 when stocks were dwindling, and the Convention was amended in 1957 to include pink salmon as well as sockeyes. It is a Canada-United States agreement, and the big and orderly annual runs of sockeyes and pinks are the best evidence of success.

Improved equipment and fishing techniques brought major changes to the industry, but most of the salmon finding their way into commercial channels are caught by one of three methods: gillnetting, seine netting, or trolling. In each case, the fisherman operates from a powerboat. A 1,200-foot gillnet drawn behind a boat is commonly operated by one man who draws it in periodically during a night of fishing and removes the captive fish. A seine boat crew, generally six or eight men, lays out its long curtain-like net to form a circular trap. The uppermost edge of the net is held to the surface by floats, and the lower edge, suspended deep in the water, is furnished with a draw-cord, which, when pulled, makes the net resemble a big sack, and fish on the inside have no way to escape. The fish are then removed to the boat. On the other hand, the troller, as the name suggests, depends upon long lines baited with spoons and hooks, very much as a sport fisherman might use.

In British Columbia fishing circles, people talk about the five kinds of salmon: pink, sockeye, cohoe, chum, and spring. All are beautiful and valuable. In the annual amount canned, they rank in the above order. The 1963 pack, totalling 1,203,271 cases, showed pink salmon with 757,453 cases, sockeyes with 158,375, cohoes with 157,481, chums with 119,000, and springs with 10,000 cases.

The five differ somewhat in life history, but all are born in fresh water and, after spending varying lengths of time there, they go to the ocean. Eggs are laid in gravel beds, as far as 600 miles from the sea, and hatch during the winter, often under the ice. Toward spring, the small things, with big eyes and sac-like appendages, emerge from the shelter of gravel bars and swim around in the river or lake water.

The sockeyes, most valuable of the five kinds for canning, remain in the freshwater lake for at least a year, and then, as fingerlings, start downstream to the ocean. No one knows where they go in the broad Pacific, but in the sockeye's third year at sea, it develops a compulsive urge to return to the place where it was born, there to complete its life's purpose. The journey may be long and dangerous but, unerringly, the mature salmon must make its way to the mouth of the river from which it entered the ocean, and then, against currents and other obstacles, it must get back to its native gravel for spawning and dying. The journey may be exhausting, but the salmon does not give up. Finally, having completed a predetermined life cycle, a four-year span in the case of the sockeye, the adults enter into the business of egg laying, and then, quite promptly, they die. Pink salmon live only two years, but spend a bigger proportion of their lives in the ocean. Normally, the cohoe has a life span of three years, and the big spring salmon lives four or five years. The length of life varies with the species, but the pattern is roughly the same for all, filled with wonder and danger.

The salmon has been described as Canada's most mysterious and most fascinating natural resource. It is a self-renewing resource when given a chance, requiring only natural habitat and reasonable restraint on the part of fishermen.

The Fraser River system came to be recognized as the world's greatest source of salmon. Unfortunately, the industry did not escape some disastrous experiences, the most notable of which was in 1913 and 1914 when railroad builders allowed some millions of tons of rock to fall into the narrow river gorge at Hell's Gate Canyon. It was enough to block the upstream migrations of sockeyes and pinks and served to reduce the annual harvest seriously. Steps were taken to clear the river partially, however, and to install fishways or fishladders, and the recovery was encouraging.

The British Columbia herring is a smaller fish, about a foot long at maturity, but it ranks second in importance to the salmon. Its use is varied: some of the annual herring catch is canned, some kippered or smoked, and some reduced to oil and fishmeal for feed to livestock.

Halibut, ranking third in the British Columbia operations, has been a favourite ever since white men came upon the scene. It is found at great depths off Vancouver Island's west coast and north along the mainland and Queen Charlotte Islands. Described as a flatfish, the halibut is big. Mature females, weighing up to 200 and 300 pounds, only start to spawn at 10 or 11 years of age. Fishing for halibut is rigidly controlled in order to protect the species, and the International Pacific Halibut Convention, to which Canada and the United States are parties, is another example of cooperation by countries with similar interests in resource conservation.

Fishermen with the huge seine nets being pulled on board off the fishing grounds of San Juan, B.C.

Pacific Ocean fishing quite overshadows freshwater fishing as conducted in the midwestern provinces. Nevertheless, fishing in Manitoba, Saskatchewan, and Alberta lakes employs some 10,000 or more people and is not to be overlooked. Manitoba has 40,000 square miles of freshwater lakes, with Lake Winnipeg accounting for about a quarter of the total. That lake has been a dependable source of commercial fish ever since the Icelandic immigrants chose the area for farming and fishing in 1875. As a result, Manitoba leads the midwestern provinces in the value of fish landed annually. The figure for 1962 showed Manitoba with 36,105,000 pounds of fish, Saskatchewan with 14,999,000 pounds, and Alberta with 9,025,000 pounds.

Fish should be seen as a renewable resource and, with good management, Canadians can be rich in fish resources forever.

Fortune in Forests

Forestry became an important industry in most provinces, especially in British Columbia, where the topography precluded large scale farming, and heavy precipitation in mountain and coastal regions favoured the growth of big trees of valuable kinds, such as Douglas fir, cedar, spruce, hemlock, and pine. Just as agricultural soil was Nature's finest gift to the midwestern part of Canada, so was the forest to British Columbia.

Trees have always been mankind's friends, furnishing shelter, fuel, building materials, weapons like bows and arrows, furniture, posts, paper, fruit, recreation and, now, synthetic articles in a thousand forms. Forest products are surpassed only by food products from agriculture in their importance to the human family.

It is not to be overlooked that Canada is a forest country, with about half of all its land supporting trees. Of the nation's 3,560,000 square miles of land area, 1,714,000 square miles, or just over a billion acres, are forested to one degree or another. It does not mean that all tree-covered land is growing saleable wood, but enough of it is classified as productive to give the country's pulp mills and saw mills a place of prominence in Canadian industry.

Anyone studying Canadian forestry must be prepared for big figures. The annual harvest, for example, averages more than three billion cubic feet; enough wood, according to a federal government estimate, to provide a platform twenty-four feet wide and one foot thick completely around the world at the equator. Ninety per cent of the annual cut is in the form of sawlogs and pulpwood.

While the Canadian wheat exports in 1966 would be worth about a billion dollars, the value of forest products exported would be almost two billion. This illustrates how much the forest industries mean to national economy. Even in furnishing employment, the forest industry is the leader. Operations in the woods, lumber mills, pulp and paper plants, and wood-using factories provide jobs for some 300,000 Canadians. The biggest single group works in the forests, where the equivalent of 80,000 people is required on a year-round basis.

At one time, forestry meant only wood for fuel and logs for building shelters. The first wood articles for export from Canadian shores consisted of masts for ships, barrel staves for the West Indies rum trade, and pine timbers squared with broadaxes wielded by skilful hands. As time passed, the forests yielded an ever wider range of wood materials: lumber, wood pulp, Christmas trees, maple syrup, turpentine, and many other useful articles.

Indians on the west coast used cedar logs in making totem poles, dugout canoes, and houses, but the white man saw the huge trees as something he could sell as well as use. A sawmill was placed in operation on Millstream, close to Victoria, in 1848, just two years after the Oregon Boundary dispute was settled and five years after the new fort built on Vancouver Island was christened Victoria. Almost at once, the new mill was furnishing lumber for shipment to Fort Langley and San Francisco, and more mills were started at other coastal locations to which logs could be floated and from which lumber could be loaded on ocean-going boats or barges.

In this early period, logging was conducted by the most primitive and laborious methods. Cutting was done with hand axes and cross-cut saws; workers accepted humble living quarters and dietary fare dominated by baked beans and fat pork. Heavy logs were dragged from the woods by multiple ox teams driven tandem. Waste left in the forest was shockingly high; however, new methods were introduced gradually. Power-driven chain saws displaced the hand tools; logging roads were built to areas once considered inaccessible; caterpillar tractors and heavy logging trucks took the place of oxen and bush horses.

By 1963, the total Canadian cut was 3,660,365,000 cubic feet, and the British Columbia share represented 44 per cent of the national total. Alberta's cut in the same year accounted for a little less than four per cent, and Saskatchewan and Manitoba had about one per cent each.

A British Columbia forest setting, representing a fraction of western wealth in lumber and its by-products.

National Film Board

The province of Quebec became the Canadian leader in pulp production, and in a recent year, it accounted for 38 per cent of the total tonnage, while Ontario produced 24 per cent and British Columbia 20 per cent. Canadian forests brought this country to a foremost world position as a supplier of pulp and paper. Beginning with a pulp plant built in the year before Confederation, the industry grew to become a giant, ranking first in value of its output and exports, and first as an employer of labour. In recent years, while lumber accounted for approximately one-quarter of the total value of all wood products exported, pulp and paper were responsible for two-thirds.

In lumber, however, British Columbia was the national leader, showing a 1963 production value of $477,983,000, which was about 70 per cent of the Canadian total. It was an impressive share, and more could be told about British Columbia's part in manufacturing plywood, chipboard, and similar composite wood materials being used in building.

Forest administration is a provincial responsibility, and there is a striking similarity in the policies followed across the nation. All provinces are now seeking to conduct forest operations in such a manner that the harvest will never diminish. British Columbia, recognizing the special importance of its forests, was particularly aggressive in adopting management principles which would minimize losses from forest fires, tree insects, and disease, bring sensible control to cutting, and reduce the familiar waste in the woods as much as possible. The objective of sustained yield could not be achieved without the cooperation of all segments of the industry. The Tree Farm Licence, an agreement between the government and forest operators, was something which would bind the latter to manage a designated forest area in such a way that productivity would not decline. It was considered a success.

Coupled with such management policies, British Columbia embarked upon an ambitious program of reforestation by planting seedling trees in areas where natural regeneration was backward. Lumber companies cooperated, and millions of young trees were transferred annually from forest nurseries to rugged woodlands.

Canadians who once feared that the rate of cutting and burning would lead to depletion of forests found reason for comfort. As a result of thoughtful management, it could be reported that the Canadian utilization of 3,432,000,000 cubic feet of forest wood in a recent year represented less than half of one per cent of total Canadian supply as shown by the National Forest Inventory. Although the forests of British Columbia and other parts of Canada have supported industry for many years, the benefits derived from their yield will continue, thanks to the policies of conservation and careful handling which now prevail.

Millions From Mines

Even at the time of King Solomon, any country having mines from which to draw wealth in useful and valuable minerals commanded the envy of neighbours. The only trouble, as the ancient Greeks and Romans discovered, was that minerals were non-renewable and could become depleted.

Mining was one of Canada's early industries. Jacques Cartier, on his visit to the St. Lawrence River in 1536, saw copper in the hands of local Indians and heard the native people tell about the Kingdom of Saguenay where gold and silver were to be found in abundance. Using bog iron deposits in the St. Maurice River Valley of Quebec, settlers started a smelter, and for more than a hundred years after 1737, it was a source of iron for the making of pots, cannon balls, and plowshares.

The West and Northwest, like the East, inherited a rich legacy of minerals, but it was relatively late in being recognized. When Palliser conducted his famous survey, the West was still seen as an area lacking resources other than soil, forests, and wild life. True, Samuel Hearne saw copper on the Coppermine River in the far North in 1772, and Alexander Mackenzie, on his journey to the Arctic in 1789, noticed traces of oil at points along the river. Moreover, Hudson's Bay Company men were mining coal on Vancouver Island as early as 1835, but the western half of British North America continued to be regarded as a vast and barren land.

British Columbia prospectors were the first to make important mineral discoveries. They found gold on the Lower Fraser in 1858 and saw successive events lead to a gold rush. Scarcely had the gold rush ended, when base metals were discovered in southeastern British Columbia. Copper and gold were found at Rossland in 1889, and the well-known Sullivan mine at Kimberley, destined to become one of the world's biggest producers of lead, zinc, and silver, was in production in 1895. By 1898, when the gold rush was on to the Klondike, British Columbia's southeastern section was flourishing from mining.

The Canadian Pacific Railway acquired a smelter at Trail in 1898 and found added reason for building the Crow's Nest Pass Railway which would bring needed coal from mines in the pass to heat the smelters. In 1910, the Canadian Pacific bought the Sullivan Mine and, in so doing, helped to make Trail a mining centre of national and international importance. From Trail came lead, zinc, silver, cadmium, bismuth, antimony, gold, and many kinds of fertilizers for shipment to distant parts of the world.

British Columbia prospectors found mineral wealth in various other sections: silver, lead, and zinc in the Slocan area, copper at Howe Sound, silver in the north, and so on. Production rose steadily until, in 1966, the value of British Columbia's mineral output stood at $331,700,000. Of this total, $209,650,000 came from metals, meaning gold, silver, copper, lead, zinc, iron, cadmium, nickel, and molybdenum; $22,900,000 of the total came from industrial minerals such as asbestos and sulphur; $37,900,000 came from structural materials like cement, sand, and gravel; and $61,-250,000 came from mineral fuels, namely coal, oil, and natural gas.

In the Alberta area, the pioneer mining effort was with coal, and the story began in 1870 when Nicholas Sheran, travelling from Fort Benton, Montana, to Fort Whoop-Up, a few miles southwest of today's Lethbridge, saw outcroppings of coal along the banks of St. Mary River. He built a shack near Whoop-Up, operated a ferry, and then found a richer seam of coal at a point on the Oldman River, beside the present city of Lethbridge. There he engaged in coal mining and saw his coal loaded on wagons to be hauled by bull-teams to Fort Benton, 200 miles away. When the Mounted Police established themselves at Fort Macleod, they obtained their winter fuel supplies at Sheran's mine, paying $3 per ton for the coal.

A cairn at Lethbridge pays honour to the pioneer enterprise. The plaque records the achievement in these words: "In 1872, on the western bank of the Oldman River, at the present site of the Federal Mine, Nicholas Sheran

The town of Flin Flon, with the Hudson's Bay Mining and Smelting complex in the background.

George Hunter for H.B.M. and S.

opened the first coal mine in Alberta. He broke his own trails, found his own markets and hauled coal by ox-team 200 miles to Fort Benton, Montana, and other distant points. Thus was founded a vital industry that has contributed greatly to the development and welfare of Western Canada."

The importance of coal in Canadian industry rose and fell, but Alberta was left with almost half of the nation's estimated hundred billion tons of reserve, sooner or later to be put to useful purpose.

For many years, the Hudson's Bay Mining and Smelting Company mine at Flin Flon was the leading operation of its kind in the Manitoba-Saskatchewan area. Located in a relatively remote part of Manitoba, 400 air miles from Winnipeg and 400 air miles from Churchill, Flin Flon obtained its name from Tom Creighton, pioneer prospector of the North, who drove the stakes to mark the discovery of the extensive copper-zinc deposits in 1915. Creighton and fellow prospectors had been reading a dime novel entitled *Sunless City*, by J. Preston Murdock. The leading character in the story, Josiah Flintabatty Flonatin, with a submarine of his own making, undertook to explore a bottomless lake. After travelling straight down through the lake water for two weeks, he came upon a subterranean world having mountains of pure gold. Before Flonatin could stake claims on the precious ore, however, he was captured by the women rulers of that lower region. It was only when he crawled up and out through the crater of an extinct volcano that he was able to escape. As a result, when Tom Creighton came upon a circular hole in his claim, he supposed it might be the crater from which Flonatin escaped from the women's world. Accordingly, he would call the place "Flin Flon", and the name remained to be adopted when the mining town arose.

Hudson's Bay Mining and Smelting Company was formed in 1926, while neither town nor railway existed in that rocky part. Preparations for mining were begun in 1928, and after pumping out a lake and removing a million tons of mud and clay overburden, the company was ready for operations in 1930. Ore from the top 300 feet was mined by open-pit methods, while that at lower levels was taken by means of the conventional shafts. Recovery from that well-known mine included copper, zinc, gold, silver, cadmium, selenium, and tellurium.

To give Flin Flon added distinction, it straddled the border between Manitoba and Saskatchewan. Operations began on the Manitoba side, but digging and blasting led into underground Saskatchewan. The provincial boundary was marked at underground levels as well as at the surface, and both provinces collected royalties on ore. There were some unusual circumstances, as when a workman fell from a point on the Manitoba side and was injured by landing on the floor of a shaft on the Saskatchewan side and nobody was sure which province should be expected to pay workman's compensation.

Flin Flon, once the most northerly mining centre in Manitoba, lost that distinction. The Sherritt Gordon Mine at Sherridon developed from a discovery in 1922, and when ore at that point began to fail, the equipment and even housing were moved farther north to Lynn Lake where nickel and copper were present in abundance.

Right across the country, the search for minerals was pressed northward. Manitoba saw nickel coming from Thompson and Rankin Inlet, uranium deposits in Saskatchewan's northwest corner were attracting greater attention, and Albertans were taking stock of their biggest reserves of oil in the Rainbow area and the oil sands at McMurray and anticipating an iron mining development in their Northwest.

Still farther north, in the Yukon and the Northwest Territories, the mining potential gave ever greater evidence of being fabulous. Prospectors must have thought so too when claims recorded in 1966 showed 22,443 in the Northwest Territories and 15,708 in the Yukon. Some indication of what may yet be found could be gained by noting the gold reserves at Yellowknife, silver at Keno, iron ore in the northern Yukon, uranium at Great Bear Lake, more iron ore in undetermined amounts on Baffin Island, oil at Norman Wells, asbestos north of Dawson City, zinc-silver-lead deposits northwest of Whitehorse, and lead-zinc treasure at Pine Point.

According to the *Canada Year Book, 1966*, on page 550, "Canada is the world's largest diversified exporter of minerals and metals and follows the United States and the Soviet Union as a mineral producing nation."

It is a story of ever-expanding industry. Canadian mines in the year 1900 yielded $64,000,000 worth of minerals. The output climbed to a value of a billion dollars for the first time in 1950. By 1965, it exceeded three and one-half billion dollars. Ontario continued to lead the provinces in production, accounting for 26 per cent of the Canadian total in 1965. Alberta was second with 21 per cent, and Quebec was third with 19 per cent of the national total.

The same records showed Ontario, Quebec, British Columbia, and Saskatchewan respectively to be the leaders in copper production. Quebec, Newfoundland, Ontario, and British Columbia led in iron ore. British Columbia, then Newfoundland, the Yukon, and Manitoba produced the most lead. Ontario and Manitoba were far ahead of other provinces in nickel, making Canada the foremost world supplier of that mineral. Incidentally, about three-quarters of all the nickel in international trade originates in Canadian mines. Ontario and Manitoba were the leading producers of cobalt in the year noted. Ontario and Saskatchewan led in uranium; Ontario, British Columbia, and Yukon in silver; Quebec, British Columbia, and Ontario in asbestos; Saskatchewan in potash; Ontario, Nova Scotia, and Alberta in salt; Alberta in sulphur; Nova Scotia, Alberta, and Saskatchewan in coal; Alberta, British Columbia, and Saskatchewan in natural gas; Alberta, Saskatchewan, and British Columbia in oil; and Saskatchewan in sodium sulphate.

Taken together, these varied minerals furnish added proof of Canada's good fortune in natural resources.

Oil and Gas Reshape the Economy

For purposes of statistics, oil and gas classify as minerals and are grouped with gold, copper, and iron ore. For people in the western provinces, however, there is something special about these products which reshaped the country's economy, justifying special treatment in any account of the West.

February 13, 1947, when oil was discovered at Leduc, must be seen as the most important single date in western Canada's industrial history. It marked success after long and costly searching and started Canada on the way from oil poverty to oil riches. For the Imperial Oil Company, after drilling 133 consecutive dry holes, this, the 134th well, was the rewarding one about which men had been dreaming.

It was not the first oil discovery in Canada. The first for Canada, and also the first on the continent, was at Oil Springs, Ontario, in 1858, and there was the oil strike at Alberta's Turner Valley in 1914. Actually, the story might very properly begin long before these dates because the ever-coveted oil and natural gas were hiding in pores of subterranean rock for at least 10 million years, some of it for an estimated 500 million years before being discovered and brought to the surface to serve man's needs.

During the eons of time the oil was in hiding deep in the earth's crust, many forms of plants and animals disappeared and new ones emerged. The climate changed from polar to tropical and back again. Glaciers advanced and receded several times to alter the face of the continent. Seas and dry land changed places, and mountains were worn down and new ones appeared.

It is perfectly clear that the face of the continent changed many times as oceans invaded and receded. Great inland seas repeatedly occupied the central part, extending from the Gulf of Mexico to the Arctic. There was the Cambrian Sea of over half a billion years ago, probably the first to have animal life in it. Capturing energy from the sun, primitive animal forms multiplied and died, and layer after layer of dead bodies went to the bottom, becoming entombed in sand and silt. As these sedimentary layers were pressed into shale and limestone, the first fossilized rock was formed, the Cambrian rock. With the passing of time, the Cambrian Sea disappeared, and after more millions of years, the Ordovician Sea came in, then the Silurian, Devonian, Cretaceous, and others.

Life was primitive but abundant, and when trapped in sediments, the organic matter underwent change without any appreciable loss of energy. In other words, it was transformed to crude oil and natural gas. But natural forces did not end at that point. Internal stresses occurred, and sedimentary rocks were shifted and twisted. Gas and oil may have been forced out of the shale in which they originated and into porous sandstone. If the porous structures extended all the way to the surface, the oil and gas would escape. If they were overlaid with impervious rock acting like a lid, the oil and gas remained undisturbed for millions of years or until ingenious man discovered the fossilized sunshine and withdrew it.

Within the boundaries of present-day Alberta, now the "Oil Province" of Canada, the first discoveries were by frontiersmen who professed no knowledge of geology. Kootenai Brown, who was squatting beside Waterton Lakes, asked the Indians if they had seen anything resembling a mixture of kerosene and molasses. He was directed to a scum of oil on intermountain water and took some of it to lubricate the axles of his wagon. About the same time, Lafayette French, who conducted a trading post in the foothills, suffered a leg wound and had an Indian woman dress the injured limb with what French identified as crude oil. He later told government surveyor A. P. Patrick about it, and together they set out to find the source or the squaw who used it. They found the lady and bribed her into leading them to the oil which happened to be beside Cameron Brook, not far from Waterton. This led to drilling and the discovery of a small amount of oil.

Meanwhile, in 1889, a natural gas strike was made at Alderson, northwest of Medicine Hat. The engineers who found it at 700 feet were actually drilling for water, but their discovery was enough to induce Medicine Hat people to probe for gas nearer home. Sure enough they found it, and ultimately used it for heating and lighting.

More important was the discovery made at Turner Valley on land owned by William Stewart Heron. Coming from Ontario, where he gained some experience in mining, Heron settled near Okotoks. When fording Sheep Creek with a wagon of coal, he noticed an oil seepage and was so fascinated by the possibilities that he bought the farm and obtained the mineral rights. In trying to interest Calgary capitalists in a drilling venture, he invited them to his ranch, then, quite casually, lit a trickle of gas close to the creek and fried eggs over the flame. The demonstration was convincing; the Calgary Petroleum Products Company was formed, and drilling was

One of Esso's rigs operating in Alberta's Rainbow Lake Field.

undertaken on Heron's land. There, on May 14, 1914, the pioneer drillers made their historic strike at a depth of 2,718 feet. That well, known as Dingman Number One, marked discovery of the first major oil field in the British Empire.

Word reached Calgary, 30 miles away, in the evening, and within hours the city was wild with enthusiasm. New companies, literally hundreds of them, were formed, and Calgary people seized the title, "Oil Capital Of Canada". World War I broke out soon after, however, and the oil boom collapsed, not to be revived for some years after war's end.

Until 1947, Turner Valley, Canada's leading oil field, was something about which to boast. It reached a production peak of 30,000 barrels a day. In spite of its importance, Turner Valley was small compared to the fields soon to be discovered. Leduc Number One, which blew in on that February day in 1947, was like the spark that "set the heather ablaze". The new field proved to be big and rich, and the oil industry responded with further exploration and big investment. New fields with proven reserves of gas and oil were discovered, and annual production soared.

Important discoveries were made in Saskatchewan and northeast British Columbia, and in 1965, a strike at Rainbow Lake, close to Alberta's northern boundary, looked as though it might make all other Canadian discoveries seem small. Men talked about the possibility of the field which would extend into British Columbia and the Northwest Territories, yielding a billion barrels of oil.

Nothing in Canada's entire catalogue of resources appeared as overwhelming as the estimates of oil in the Athabasca oil sands near Fort McMurray. Those estimates ranged to 750 billion barrels, more than the total known reserves in the Middle East. When it was noted that Canada's proven reserves in conventional oil pools in 1967 were placed at eight and one-half billion barrels, the staggering magnitude of Athabasca stores was plain.

It must have been oil from these sands that caught the eyes of Peter Pond and Alexander Mackenzie almost 200 years ago as they travelled along northern rivers. Outcroppings of the oil sands occur for a hundred miles along the Athabasca River and its tributaries. Overburden will vary in depth, but seams of the oil-bearing sand range from 150 to 175 feet in thickness, and the area of the sands extends to about 30,000 square miles.

The trouble in developing the resource was that extracting the oil promised to be difficult and too costly to be practical. For many years, scientists searched for better ways of unlocking the oil from the sand. Finally, Great Canadian Oil Sands Limited received authorization to embark upon commercial extraction. The venture was costly, but late in 1967, the synthetic crude oil began to flow from the 235 million dollar plant about 20 miles north of Fort McMurray. The initial production was set at 45,000 barrels per day.

By the time the McMurray oil was moving through the 266-mile pipeline to Edmonton, Canada's oil production had risen from eight million barrels in 1947 to almost 300 million barrels, and gas sales had shown a similar rise.

Natural gas has always moved by pipeline, but by 1967, most of the oil was moving that way. Concurrent with the expansion of the oil industry was the construction of pipelines, and by 1967, the pipeline complex, 12,000 miles of oil lines and more than 6,000 miles of gas lines, represented an investment of two billion dollars.

Most of those pipelines originated in Alberta to convey oil and gas to eastern Canada, to the west coast, and to the United States. In 1964, Alberta produced 87 per cent of Canada's natural gas and 67 per cent of the crude oil. Of the nation's 274 million barrels of oil produced in that year, 168 million barrels came from Alberta wells, 71 million barrels from Saskatchewan, 12 million from British Columbia, and four million from Manitoba. This clearly showed how far western oil and gas were meeting the nation's needs. The fact was that more than 93 per cent of oil produced in Canada during the year mentioned was from the West.

Saskatchewan's Potash

Potash was like a special bonus for Saskatchewan, an extremely rich one. There was enough potash underlying the wheat country to meet world needs for hundreds of years.

As the prairie potash wonder grew, it could not escape notice that the area from which the product was coming appeared to be one-crop country a mere 25 years earlier. It was wheat country, and when wheat failed, as it did in the thirties, there was practically nothing in the local economy upon which to rely. In the intervening years, the "Wheat Province" discovered new wealth in oil, natural gas, and metallic minerals, and then the potash appeared in unbelievable amounts to broaden the economic base substantially.

The great belt of potash extending across the province was from 3,000 to 7,000 feet below the surface, and no one could be surprised that it escaped discovery for so long. Like oil and natural gas, it was a bequest from the distant past. There, millions of years ago, the waters from a dank sea evaporated, leaving a thick deposit of salt bearing large amounts of the element potassium.

Potash, as a potassium compound, has many uses in industry, but inasmuch as it is one of the essential plant foods, its most important use is in agriculture. Much of the world's food-producing soil is sadly deficient, and without the application of potash fertilizers, those soils would be immediately unproductive. Ironically, western Canadian soils are already well supplied with this particular plant food. Canadian statistics on fertilizer sales show that western farmers are using more and more commercial fertilizer, but they are interested almost exclusively in nitrogen and phosphate carriers rather than potash.

In most parts of the world, however, food production would suffer at once if potash fertilizer were not available. As a result, the export of Saskatchewan potash was to prove helpful and useful in relieving world hunger. A shipload of potash for application on the soil of a needy country could be of much greater value in meeting food requirements than a boatload of wheat or flour. It is possible that in the future the export of potash and other fertilizers from Canada will do more than the annual sales of wheat in overcoming the world's most pressing need. As well as adding to world food resources, this great wealth of potash may do as much for Saskatchewan's people as oil did for Alberta's.

Potash was mined in Germany in 1865 and 60 years later was discovered in New Mexico. In the years after 1925, New Mexico was meeting nearly all North American needs, but until shortly after the discovery of oil at Leduc, nobody suspected the fabulous stores of potassium chloride under the Canadian prairies. Moreover, when oil drillers working near Radville, in southern Saskatchewan, withdrew a core of potassium salts in 1943, no one was greatly impressed. Gradually, however, the extent of western Canada's potash resources became evident and the importance understood.

In 1955, Continental Potash Corporation began commercial production near Unity, in western Saskatchewan. A short time later, Potash Company of America completed a shaft at Patience Lake, near Saskatoon, at a reported cost of $25,000,000. These pioneer developers did not escape serious difficulties. First of all, there was the obvious necessity of a 3,000-foot shaft to reach the deposit. Presenting still more of an obstacle was the unanticipated necessity of sealing off water from the Blairmore sands, a 200- or 300-foot layer of water-soaked sand and silt which could flood a mine shaft. Production at the Patience Lake mine began in 1958, but the uncontrolled seepage forced a suspension of operations, and production was not resumed until 1965.

All the potash mining undertakings in Saskatchewan encountered the same Blairmore sand problem, and the cost in extra work and delay has been very great. Indeed, it was enough to induce some companies to withdraw from the Saskatchewan scene.

To overcome the water problem at Esterhazy, where the International

Ilse's Photo Studio

Potash mine near Esterhazy, Saskatchewan. The recent discovery of potash in Saskatchewan has added greatly to the province's potential in natural resources.

Minerals and Chemical Corporation began work in 1958, it was necessary to freeze the Blairmore stratum for a distance of 50 feet around the shaft and then install a 3,000-ton cast iron lining. The freezing alone took almost a year to accomplish, but the effort met with success, and the company went into production in 1962. Before the first ton of potash was offered for sale from that mine, the company was said to have invested $30,000,000 at the site.

Newer methods were brought to potash mining in Saskatchewan. Early in 1963, it was announced that Kalium Chemicals Limited would immediately start a plant which would employ the solution method of mining. It appeared to be the most practical method of getting at the deep reserves in the Belle Plaine district, west of Regina. By such a process, water is pumped down drill holes, some 5,000 feet down, in the case of the Belle Plaine operation, and when the potash has been dissolved, the solution is brought back to the surface for potash recovery. With both the conventional and solution methods of mining potash, large amounts of water are needed.

With three mines in operation in 1966, production exceeded two million tons of potash worth $75,000,000. It was expected that by 1970 the province would be furnishing 10 million tons per year, enough to meet more than half of world requirements. At such a rate of mining, how long would the Saskatchewan reserves last? Estimates of the amount of potash under Saskatchewan ranged up to 60 billion tons. There may be more. In any case, that amount would represent roughly half of the world's known reserves. If world use averages 14 million tons per year at the present time, a supply of 60 billion tons would furnish an equal amount annually for over 4,000 years.

People in Saskatoon saw their city becoming the potash capital of the world and an International Potash Show held there in October 1965 did much to strengthen the claim. The event, attended by over 1,000 industrialists with potash interests, emphasized the very great importance of the growing industry to the community, the nation, and the world. Saskatoon citizens were easily convinced of this fact.

The magnitude of the Saskatchewan potash treasure was a bit overwhelming. It suggested that long after the oil and gas have been exhausted, potash will still be produced by Saskatchewan mines and exported for agricultural and other purposes. In meeting the specific needs of overworked soils, there will never be substitutes for nitrogen, phosphate, and potash.

Today and Tomorrow

The brevity of western Canada's recorded story adds to its charm. And a short story can be a good one. Canadians visiting the Old World and seeing where Abraham was supposed to have dug a well 4,000 years ago and where Pericles was at the peak of his political power in Democratic Athens 2,400 years ago might conclude that the history of their own West, which had not completely disengaged itself from the Stone Age just 100 years ago, is relatively unimportant. Such a conclusion would be wrong. It is the achievements and events which enrich the history of a particular area rather than the years.

Western Canadians celebrating the centennial anniversary of Confederation took stock of an area quickly transformed from a wilderness to a land with super highways, fine homes, superior educational facilities, challenging opportunities, and one of the highest standards of living in the world. These phenomenal changes in so short a time could only find explanation in a combination of rich natural resources and vigorous people.

As mentioned previously, Confederation year meant practically nothing to the scattered residents of Rupert's Land. They had more reason to be interested in the policies of the Hudson's Bay Company than in the efforts of the Fathers of Confederation to bring the eastern provinces into union. For those people who had adopted the western frontier, a more meaningful landmark date might have been 1869, when the Hudson's Bay Company relinquished its territorial claims in Rupert's Land; or 1870, when the province of Manitoba was created; or 1874, when the Mounted Police trekked westward to build Fort Macleod; or 1876, when the first wheat was sent from the West; or 1878, when the first railway tracks were laid to Winnipeg.

These dates are within the lifetime of some Canadians still living today and serve to illustrate the dramatic changes which took place in only a few decades. But the winning of the West was not easy. Pioneer years were trying in many ways, and there were many tests to be undergone. Some of the reverses were serious and might well have been more serious. Indian hostility posed a grave danger for some years; twice there was something resembling rebellion; and twice there was involvement in world wars. There was no greater blow to local progress than the years of extreme drought which accompanied the depression in the thirties and cast undisguised gloom and pessimism over a land which had been gaining fame for hope and optimism.

But crises were interspersed with triumphs. The country judged to be doomed to eternal sterility was found to be a virtual treasure chest of resources. The area George Simpson considered to be unsuited to cultivation because of the poverty of its soil turned out to be one of the world's best for food production. The privately-owned piece of real estate known as Rupert's Land, with no recognized future except in producing furs, was found to hold unbelievable riches such as gold, iron, oil, natural gas, coal, and potash, all of which added much to the area's economy.

It was not a country for faint hearts. There were those individuals who could not endure the frontier hardships and disappointments and who, with a sense of relief, moved to other regions where life was easier and more secure. Others, however, with determination and muscle and fibre, remained to impart to the frontier its vigorous character. To the resources like soil, forests, gas, and oil, of which Westerners were able to boast, one must add the priceless quality of pioneer fortitude supported by self-reliance and energy.

The change, of course, went far beyond the mere recovery of natural resources. In 1967, viewers of the western scene saw factories and industries of many kinds, contradicting the old dictum that "the West can grow the wheat; the East will keep the factories". With raw materials and the necessary skills, it could have been expected that diversified industry would emerge. The earliest manufacturing had its base in agriculture, forestry, and fishing. Understandably, the plants were abattoirs, flour mills, creameries, tanneries, saw mills, and canning establishments. With a higher level of production and a bigger population, however, factories became more varied and more numerous.

One of the best indications of the growth in manufacturing was the increasing demand for electrical power. Between 1947 and 1967, the use of electrical energy increased by 300 per cent. The Portage Mountain project in British Columbia, the complex Columbia River development, and the South Saskatchewan River operation, each of which cost a staggering amount of money, symbolized the change to a more advanced and complex economy.

But what of tomorrow? Is it inevitable that progress will continue in an uninterrupted manner as in recent years? Success gives no reason for complacency. Time and again throughout history smugness has been the forerunner of decline. Too often people who had the courage and will to cope with difficult pioneer problems failed in dealing with the problems accompanying success and wealth. Progress can and should continue, but there is no guarantee that it will. As long as natural and human resources last, progress and prosperity will likely go hand in hand with them. But for how long can they be expected to survive? All Canadians must be on guard to preserve those qualities which brought them to positions of comfort.

As for the natural resources, some of them will not last forever; indeed, some will not last many years. With proper care, the renewable resources may last forever. Regardless of early greed and waste in handling forests, the new policies based on sustained yield are sound and will win the approval of Canadians a hundred years hence. Likewise, the concern for soil in relation to world food needs should ensure safeguards for Canada's most precious natural asset. With understanding care, agricultural soils can be as productive in a thousand years' time as they have been in recent years, and the world's growing population will bring ever greater importance to those soils. Similarly, it has been proven that fish resources will respond to intelligent management.

Such, however, is not the case with certain other resources described as non-renewables: oil, natural gas, minerals from the mines. These should be used with the realization that waste and extravagance may mean depriving Canadians of a later generation of something to which they will feel they have a claim. They are easy to destroy and may be impossible to restore.

Any one with concern for the future of his land must think seriously about protection for wild life, safeguards for forests, arresting soil depletion and erosion, prevention of pollution in air and water, preservation of parkland, and the minimizing of waste in all resources, none of which is inexhaustible.

Index

Agriculture, 61, 123, 127, 128, 138-142
Alberta, 4, 17, 114, 117, 119, 134, 138, 145, 157
Allan, Hugh, 94
Anglican Church, 45
Archibald, Lt.-Gov. Adams, 77
Assiniboine Indians, 15, 17
Athabasca River, 5
Automobiles, 116

Baker, I.G., Company, 18, 105, 106
Badlands, 10
Barkerville, 64
Barr Colony, 101
Battleford, 37, 92, 95, 117
Beaver Indians, 13
Begbie, Matthew B., 60, 77
Bella Coola, 13
Big Bear, 81, 111-113
Blackfoot, 13, 15-17, 81, 90
Blackfoot Treaty Number Seven, 16, 90, 91
Blood Indians, 13, 16, 26, 90
Borden, Robert, 122
Bow River, 15, 16
Brisebois, Inspector, 96
British Columbia, 58, 61, 68, 77, 79, 93, 96, 114, 132, 144, 147, 148
British North America Act, 76
Brown, John George "Kootenai", 69, 154
Buffalo, 14, 15, 18, 20, 105, 110
Buffalo bones, 19
Buffalo Hunt, 50-53
Bulyea, G.H.V., 120
Butler, William Francis, 80

Calgary, 2, 4, 17, 19, 38, 96, 156
Calgary Herald, 108
Cameron, J.A. "Cariboo", 65
Canadian Northern Railway, 38, 98
Canadian Pacific Railway, 19, 85, 100, 112
Canadian Wheat Board, 123, 127
Cariboo, 62, 80
Cariboo Trail, 66
Cartier, Jacques, 22
Cattle, 47, 48, 85-88
Charles II, King, 23
Chesterfield House, 29
Chilcotin, 13
Chipewyan, 13
Climate, 3, 4
Cochrane, M.H., 105
Cochrane Ranch, 106
Cody, Buffalo Bill, 18
Coal, 5, 150
Cobalt, 152
Colonist, 78, 107
Columbia River, 59, 162
Confederation, 67
Cook, Capt. James, 30, 50, 142
Copper, 149, 151

Countess of Dufferin, 33
Craigellachie, 97
Cree Indians, 13, 15, 24, 81
Crozier, Major, 111
Crowfoot, Chief, 16, 84, 89, 90, 111
Cumberland House, 26, 37
Custer Massacre, 85
Cypress Hills, 56
Cypress Hills Massacre, 81

Davin, Nicholas Flood, 118
Davis, N.F., 118
de Cosmos, Amor, 77-79, 107
de la Corne, Chevalier, 25
Denis, Col. J.S., 98
Depression, 127, 130
Dinosaurs, 8, 11
Dominion Lands Act, 99
Douglas, James, 60, 77
Drought, 128-130
Drumheller, 8
Dufferin, Lord, 96
Dumont, Gabriel, 110, 111, 113
Doukhobors, 102

Edmonton, 2, 32, 33, 38, 120, 157
Edmonton Bulletin, 38, 108
Education, 134-138
Edwards, Bob, 121
Elk Island Park, 20
Eskimo, 22
Esterhazy, 158
Eye Opener, 121

Farms, 139
Fiddler, Peter, 29, 40, 47
Fishing, 142-145
Fleming, Sandford, 95
Flin Flon, 151
Forestry, 145-148
Forget, A.E., 120
Fort Albany, 23
Fort Astoria, 59
Fort Augustus, 32, 35
Fort Benton, 18, 81
Fort Charles, 23
Fort Chipewyan, 27
Fort Churchill, 23, 24
Fort Calgary, 23, 24
Fort Carlton, 18, 37, 55
Fort Dauphin, 24
Fort Douglas, 42
Fort Dunvegin, 29
Fort Edmonton, 18, 32, 35, 36, 37, 55, 56, 68, 95
Fort Fraser, 30
Fort Garry, 32, 33, 36, 49, 50, 54, 55, 68, 74, 75
Fort George, 30
Fort la Corne, 37
Fort Langley, 59
Fort la Reine, 24
Fort McMurray, 156
Fort Macleod, 4, 17, 18, 82, 84, 89

Fort Maurepas, 24
Fort Nelson, 23
Fort Pitt, 37
Fort Prince of Wales, 23, 24, 41
Fort Qu'Appelle, 17
Fort Rouge, 24, 32
Fort St. Charles, 24
Fort St. James, 30
Fort St. Pierre, 24
Fort Saskatchewan, 38, 84
Fort Vermilion, 29
Fort Victoria, 59
Fort Walsh, 82, 84
Fort Whoop-Up, 69, 83
Fraser, Simon, 27, 28, 59
Fraser River, 63
French, Commissioner G.A., 83
Frobisher, Joseph, 27
Frog Lake Massacre, 111
Fruit Production, 141
Fur trade, 22

Gaff, J.A., 18
Germans, 100
Gold, 60, 85, 149
Gold Rush, 61-66
Grand Portage, 27
Grand Trunk, 98
Grant, Cuthbert, 43, 51
Greaves, Joseph, 103, 104
Greenway, Thomas, 114
Groseilliers, 23

Haida Indians, 13
Harper Brothers, 103
Haultain, Frederick, 114, 117-120
Hearne, Samuel, 26, 149
Hell's Gate Canyon, 144
Henday, Anthony, 25, 26, 67
Hind, Henry Youle, 53, 54
Horses, 15, 46, 47
Hudson, Henry, 22
Hudson's Bay, 22
Hudson's Bay Company, 23, 26, 28, 30, 32, 33, 39, 42, 45, 48, 54, 59, 61, 68, 73, 76, 100, 107
Hudson Bay Mining and Smelting Company, 151
Hughes, Sam, 121
Hungarians, 101

Immigrants, 102
Indians, 13
Indian Treaties, 89
Iron Ore, 152
Irrigation, 139, 140

Jarvis, W.D., 37, 83
Jews, 101

Kelsey, Henry, 24
Kicking Horse Pass, 95
King, Mackenzie, 131, 132
Kootenay Indians, 13

Lagimodière, Jean Baptiste, 44, 74
Lake Athabasca, 27

Laird, Lt.-Gov. David, 89, 117
Lake Superior, 23, 24
Lane, George, 105
Laurie, Patrick Gammie, 107, 108, 119, 122
Laurier, Sir Wilfrid, 20, 114
la Vérendrye, 24, 25
Lead, 149
Leduc, 138
Lesser Slave Lake, 17
Lethbridge, 150
Luxton, Norman, 20
Lynn Lake, 152

Macdonell, Miles, 40, 42, 44, 47
Macdonald, Sir John A., 75, 79, 93, 96, 110, 112
Mackenzie, Alexander, 27, 28, 58, 94, 156
Mackenzie and Mann, 98
Mackenzie River, 5, 12
Macleod, Col. James F., 82, 83, 89
Macleod Gazette, 108
McDougall, John, 17, 70
McDougall, William, 74
McGill, James, 27
McTavish, Simon, 27
McTavish, William, 75
Manitoba, 7, 76, 100, 114, 134, 138, 145, 157
Manitoba Free Press, 108
Massacre of Seven Oaks, 42, 43
Medicine Hat, 3, 12, 154
Mennonites, 99
Métis, 42, 43, 50, 51, 55, 73, 77, 99, 110-113
Middleton, General, 112, 113
Milk River, 4
Mining, 149-153
Missionaries, 70
Moberly, Walter, 77
Moose Factory, 23
Mormons, 101
Musgrave, Anthony, 79

New Nation, 75
Nickel, 5, 152
Nootka, 13
North West Cattle Company, 105, 106
Nor'-Wester, 75, 107
North Saskatchewan, 55
North West Company, 27, 28, 30, 32, 33, 39, 40, 42-45, 47, 59
North West Mounted Police, 17, 18, 37, 81, 82, 95, 111, 161
Northwest Navigation Company, 37
North West Territories, 2, 114
North West Territories Act, 117

Oats, 141
Oil and gas, 5, 152-157
Okanagan Valley, 61
Oldman River, 69
Oliver, Frank, 107, 108
Onderdonk, Andrew, 97

Oregon Boundary Dispute, 146
Otter, Colonel, 113
Overlanders, 62, 63
Oxley Ranch, 106

Pacific Furs, 59
Pacific Scandal, 94
Palliser, John, 3, 54, 58, 72, 142
Palliser Report, 55, 58
Palliser Triangle, 56, 128
Patience Lake, 158
Peace River, 5
Pembina, 75
Pemmican, 50-53, 63
Perley, W.D., 118
Piegan, 13, 16, 90
Piegan Post, 29
Pond, Peter, 27, 30, 156
Poundmaker, 111, 113
Population, 2
Potash, 5, 6, 157-160
Potts, Jerry, 81, 83
Prairie Farm Rehabilitation Act, 139, 140
Prince Albert, 37
Prince Rupert, 23
Provincial Autonomy, 118

Quebec City, 23
Queen Charlotte Islands, 62
Quorn Ranch, 106

Radisson, Pierre, 22
Ralston, Colonel J.L., 132
Ranching, 7, 102-107
Rapeseed, 141
Red Deer River, 8, 9, 26
Red River, 32, 55, 74
Red River carts, 54, 55, 67
Regina, 19, 120
Republic of Caledonia, 71
Riel, Louis, 74, 76, 77, 98, 108, 111-113
Robson, John, 107
Rocky Mountain House, 28
Rocky Mountains, 11
Roman Catholic Church, 45
Rowand, John, 35, 36
Rupert's Land, 22, 68, 72, 161
Rupert's Land Act, 73
Russia, 59, 68
Russian thistles, 129
Rutherford, A.C., 120

Salish, 13
Sarcee, 13, 16, 90
Saskatchewan, 7, 17, 114, 117, 119, 134, 138, 141, 145, 157
Saskatchewan Herald, 108
Saskatchewan River, 18
Saskatoon, 20, 160
Scandinavian, 101
Schools, 134-138
Scott, Thomas, 75
Scott, Walter, 120
Schultz, Dr. John, 107
Selkirk, Lord, 39, 40, 44, 45

Selkirk Settlers, 32
Semlin, C.A., 114
Semple, Robert, 42, 43
Simpson, George, 30, 32, 36, 51, 72, 161
Sheep, 48, 49, 104
Sifton, Clifford, 102, 116
Silver, 149
Sioux, 13, 48, 85
Sitting Bull, 38, 85
Slaves, 13
Smallpox, 99
Smith, Donald, (Lord Strathcona), 15, 97
Snake Indians, 15
Soil, 6, 7
South Saskatchewan River, 5, 162
Spence, Thomas, 71, 72
Sternberg, C.N., 9
Stoney Indians, 13, 16, 90
Strange, General, 113
Swan River, 19

Taché, Bishop, 72
Territorial Grain Growers' Association, 124
The Pas, 25
Thompson, David, 28, 29, 59
Tree Farm license, 148
Turner Valley, 153, 156
Tyrell, Dr. J.B., 9

Ukrainians, 102
United Farmers of Alberta, 124
United States, 68, 78
Universities, 137
Uranium, 152

Vancouver, 98
Vancouver, Captain, 58
Vancouver Island Colony, 77
Van Horne, William, 95, 96, 112

Wainwright, 20
Walker, James, 105
Walking Buffalo, 16
Walrond Ranch, 106
Ware, John, 106, 116
Waterton Lakes, 69
Weapons, 13
Wheat, 88, 89, 117, 123-128, 133
Wheat Pools, 124-127
Winnipeg, 32, 33, 38, 95, 100
Winnipeg and Western Transportation Company, 37
Winnipeg Grain Exchange, 123, 127
Wolseley, Colonel Garnet, 76
Wood Buffalo Park, 20
Wood, Henry Wise, 124
Wood, C.E.D., 108, 109
World War I, 120-123
World War II, 130-133

Yellowhead Pass, 63, 95
York Factory, 25, 41

Zinc, 149, 151